PRUNING
TREES, SHRUBS AND CLIMBERS,
HEDGES, ROSES, FLOWERS AND TOPIARY

PRUNING
TREES, SHRUBS AND CLIMBERS, HEDGES, ROSES, FLOWERS AND TOPIARY

A gardener's guide to cutting, trimming and training, with over 650 photographs and illustrations, and practical, easy-to-follow advice

RICHARD BIRD

southwater

Dedication
To Hilary with lots and lots of love

This edition is published by Southwater

Southwater is an imprint of Anness Publishing Ltd
Hermes House, 88–89 Blackfriars Road, London SE1 8HA
tel. 020 7401 2077; fax 020 7633 9499;
www.southwaterbooks.com; www.annesspublishing.com

If you like the images in this book and would like to investigate using them for publishing,
promotions or advertising, please visit our website www.practicalpictures.com for more information.

© Anness Publishing Ltd 2006

UK agent: The Manning Partnership Ltd, 6 The Old Dairy, Melcombe Road, Bath BA2 3LR
tel. 01225 478444; fax 01225 478440; sales@manning-partnership.co.uk

UK distributor: Grantham Book Services Ltd, Isaac Newton Way, Alma Park Industrial
Estate, Grantham, Lincs NG31 9SD; tel. 01476 541080; fax 01476 541061;
orders@gbs.tbs-ltd.co.uk

North American agent/distributor: National Book Network, 4501 Forbes Boulevard,
Suite 200, Lanham, MD 20706; tel. 301 459 3366; fax 301 429 5746; www.nbnbooks.com

Australian agent/distributor: Pan Macmillan Australia, Level 18, St Martins Tower, 31 Market
St, Sydney, NSW 2000; tel. 1300 135 113; fax 1300 135 103;
customer.service@macmillan.com.au

New Zealand agent/distributor: David Bateman Ltd, 30 Tarndale Grove, Off Bush Road,
Albany, Auckland; tel. (09) 415 7664; fax (09) 415 8892

Publisher: Joanna Lorenz
Editorial Director: Judith Simons
Executive Editor: Caroline Davison
Project Editor: Molly Perham
Designer: Michael Morey
Jacket Design: Bally Design Associates
Illustrator: Liz Pepperell
Editorial Reader: Rosanna Fairhead
Production Controller: Lee Sargent

Previously published as part of a larger volume *Pruning, Training and Topiary*

10 9 8 7 6 5 4 3 2 1

NOTES
Bracketed terms are intended for American readers.

Contents

Introduction

Pruning is one of those garden jobs that you can ignore if you wish. However, this approach will only succeed for a while, because eventually the pruning work will accumulate and it will be a huge task to sort everything out. Gardeners' neglect of pruning is not so much through dislike or boredom – as with weeding, for example – but has more to do with a fear of the unknown. Pruning is often perceived as one of the black arts of gardening, a skill that some possess, while others do not.

Of course, as with all matters connected with gardening, it is simply a matter of experience. Sitting and thinking about pruning will not improve your technique, but getting out there and doing it will. We all make mistakes at first, but nature is very forgiving and it is not often that you kill a tree or shrub by making pruning mistakes, especially as most gardeners err on the side of caution when they first set out.

In this book we aim to provide the basic techniques that will give you the confidence to pick up your secateurs (pruners) and make a start. You will not need all the information in the book because it is doubtful whether you grow everything we cover, but it should act as a guide through many a season and many a change in your garden. Above all, it is important to have a go and see how your garden improves.

LEFT This impressive garden with its wide variety of trees, shrubs and climbers shows the benefits of careful pruning.

The principles of pruning and training

Pruning is one of those jobs that most gardeners either hate or are frightened of – or both! The fear is partly because while most garden operations seem to be common sense, cutting back a shrub or tree seems to be a drastic thing to do, which will leave disastrous evidence for everyone to see if something goes wrong. It is a bit like giving someone a haircut – you would rather leave it to the professional. The other job that is also considered tricky, propagation, is not a problem, because if the seeds do not come up or the cuttings fail, who is to know? Yes, pruning is definitely a tricky thing to attempt. Or is it?

Not a magic art
Shrubs and trees have been grown for thousands of years in gardens. People have been pruning them for all that time without causing their demise. In fact, pruning, like any other garden technique, has a logic

ABOVE A delightful crab apple tree, *Malus* 'Evereste', in full flower. It has benefited from being pruned for shape, as well as for flower production.

behind it and with experience most gardeners soon learn to prune their plants without a second thought. Most of us have a limited range of plants in the garden so it is not as if you have to remember how to prune every plant that is available, just your own collection. Pruning is definitely not a magic art; everyone can soon learn to do it.

In the wild
In nature, of course, no one prunes plants. Horses may browse them and trim them tightly back, branches die and fall off, and occasionally lightning or wind lops off a branch or even fells a whole tree, Yet nearly all manage to recover, and many plants simply grow on for years undisturbed – hundreds of years in

ABOVE This flowering currant, *Ribes sanguineum* 'Pulborough Scarlet', with its mass of brilliant flowers, is kept in shape and growing vigorous by good pruning.

ABOVE *Buddleja* or butterfly bush puts on a lot of growth during the spring and summer and needs to be cut back each year.

the case of some trees – and seem to flourish magnificently with no intervention from anyone.

So why prune?

If plants do not get much pruning in the natural world, why do they need it in gardens? There are several good reasons why we should prune, especially if you remember that we are growing plants in artificial conditions and that we want them to perform at their very best. Of course, you need not prune them at all if you do not want to. Many gardeners do not prune, but you may not get the best out of your plants. Having said that, there are many trees and shrubs that do not need any regular pruning. One of the attractions of conifers, for example, is that most require no attention at all. However, there is no doubt that if you do prune, many of your trees and shrubs will look better for it. They will be shapely and productive, and will not have any dead or damaged wood to spoil their beauty.

ABOVE An attractive group of silver birches, *Betula pendula*, that might have benefited from a little more attention with initial training so that they grew more upright.

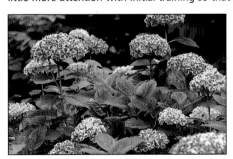

ABOVE This well-flowered hydrangea is looking at its best and has benefited from good pruning.

Reasons for pruning

Flower and fruit production – get the most out of your plants

Plant health – keep your plants healthy

Improved shape – keep the plants in the shape that you want

Control – do not let your plants take over and swamp everything

There are four main reasons for pruning. If carried out every year, the amount of work involved is often minimal and the results will greatly outweigh the effort.

Flower production

One of the main reasons for pruning is to increase the productivity of your plants. Most shrubs will produce more flowers if they are regularly pruned. Rose bushes, for example, will grow straggly if left to their own devices, with their flower power diminishing with every year that they are left unpruned. However, if they are regularly pruned so that they produce new growth, and trained so that they produce more flower buds, they will flower prolifically for many years. Some shrubs, such as *Chaenomeles*, will produce a lot more flowers if they are tightly pruned, while others, for example *Ceanothus*, do not respond well to hard pruning. Evergreen shrubs such as *Camellia* and *Osmanthus* only require pruning to keep their bushy shape.

ABOVE The layered habit of *Viburnum plicatum* is enhanced by a regime of careful pruning. This specimen has produced a large number of beautiful flowers.

Plant health

Allied to the above is the question of plant health. One of the first tasks when pruning is to remove all the dead and diseased wood. This helps keep the plant in tip-top condition and hence performing well. The very act of pruning involves looking closely at the plant, so you are likely to be much more aware of any problems. You can then take avoiding action by cutting out the diseased part. Pruning plants also prevents the branches from becoming overcrowded so that more air and light can enter, again helping to maintain a healthy plant. With shrubs in particular, it is often good practice to remove some old growth each year so that new, healthy shoots are produced, constantly rejuvenating the plant.

Improved shape

The shape of some plants, such as conifers, needs little improvement. However, there are many that benefit from being shaped: even conifers

have occasional wayward branches that need removing if their elegance is to be maintained. In the most extreme cases, hedges and topiarized plants are very heavily and regularly cut to produce a very definite ornamental shape. Most other plants

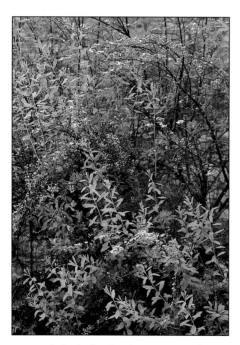

ABOVE A shrub that has been renovated may look untidy for a while, but the benefits will soon show.

ABOVE Removing dead or diseased wood helps to keep shrubs healthy and improves the production of flowers and berries.

do not need this type of intense attention but many – hollies and cherry laurel, for example – benefit from the occasional shaping.

Control

Plants have a tendency to do their own thing which may not be what the gardener wants. The soil may be richer than the plant would experience in the wild and the competition from other plants is likely to be less, so some plants go mad and ramp away. To prevent them swamping other plants or upsetting a carefully planned display, they need to be cut back. Some plants increase by running below ground and producing suckers and these will need to be removed regularly before a miniature forest develops. Shade can also be a problem, and many shrubs that have outgrown their space will need cutting back to stop them overshadowing sun-loving plants. Many climbers have a tendency to rush up a wall and enter the gutters or eaves, and these also need controlling.

ABOVE Dead wood looks ugly as well as causing further health problems for the shrub. Careful pruning can help to improve the condition of the plant.

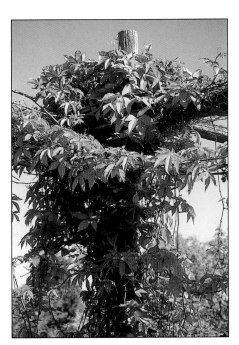

ABOVE Different types of clematis need pruning at different times of the year to ensure maximum flowering.

ABOVE Without good initial training, trees and shrubs can become misshapen and unattractive – as is the case with this camellia. While some shrubs can be cut hard back, camellias are unlikely to respond well to this, and you may need to replace it.

Tools and equipment

These can be divided into four groups. There are those that perform the cuts, such as saws, secateurs (pruners) and knives; those that are used for clearing up, such as rakes, forks and shredders; safety equipment; and finally the means to gain access to taller plants, such as ladders and towers. They can further be divided into manual tools and mechanical ones, such as hedge trimmers and chainsaws.

Cutting equipment

The most essential tool is a good pair of secateurs. These should be kept sharp. Poor-quality ones, with blades that move apart when you cut, or blunt ones, will tear the wood as it passes through. They may also crush and bruise the wood. To a skilled user, a sharp knife can replace secateurs in certain instances. For thicker wood, a pair of long-handled pruners – secateurs with long handles – can be used, but you should avoid cutting through very thick wood; use a saw instead. Long-arm pruners are secateurs on an extension arm that can reach into tall shrubs or trees but are operated from ground-level.

Saws come in a variety of shapes and sizes. Small folding saws are the most useful for the small garden owner. These are usually very sharp and remain so for some years. Instead of sharpening, as one used to do, it is usual to buy a new one when it begins to blunt. Bow saws and even chainsaws may be necessary in larger gardens. Some of the folding saws can be attached to extension arms so that higher branches can be removed without the need for ladders.

Shears are useful for hand-clipping hedges or shearing over certain shrubs such as lavender or ground cover. They are generally

LEFT Shredders are invaluable for recycling prunings of various sizes. Instead of being burnt, they are cut into small enough pieces to be composted and used again in the garden.

used for topiary where curves and trickier corners are concerned. You can also use sheep-shearing shears, but these are not the easiest things to use and scissors are easier for really intricate pieces.

Power tools

In small gardens it may be unnecessary to use power tools, but in a larger one they can be a real boon. The crucial thing about such tools is to use them sensibly. Make certain that you know how to operate them and that you are well protected. If you are uncertain about your abilities, have any work that entails their use done by professionals. Chainsaws are probably the most dangerous tool and should be used only if you have taken a course on their use. It is also very important that power tools are kept in good condition. They should be maintained professionally at least once a year. The settings and running of the engine should be checked and the cutters sharpened. Do this in advance of when you will next need them.

You can get power secateurs but these are very expensive and really useful only if you have a very large orchard and have a lot of fruit pruning or a vast amount of roses to keep in shape.

Clearing up

Most tools needed for this, such as rakes, brooms, forks, wheelbarrows and carrying sheets, should be available as part of the general garden toolkit. Another piece of power equipment of general use to the pruner is the shredder, which will reduce all the waste to small pieces suitable for composting or mulching. Electrically powered equipment is cheaper but generally less powerful and less manoeuvrable; petrol-driven machines tend to be heavier but are more mobile and therefore more suitable for larger gardens.

You also need to exercise discretion if you opt to burn prunings. Bonfires should be lit at dusk and must be supervised at all times. Check with your local council to see if there are any legal restrictions on bonfires in your area.

BASIC TOOLS AND EQUIPMENT

Most gardeners can prune the majority of their plants with just a pruning saw and a pair of secateurs (pruners), but the larger the garden and the more varied the jobs, the larger the collection of tools you will need. It is well worth investing, for example, in a long-arm chainsaw or hedge trimmer if you have tall hedges or trees that need tackling.

Curved saw with hook for removing cut-off branches

Secateurs (pruners)

Straight-bladed pruning saw

Curved pruning saw

Long-arm pruners

Shredder

Hand shears with a wavy blade

Long-handled pruners

Long-arm chainsaw

Hand shears with a straight blade

Petrol hedge trimmer

Electric hedge trimmer

Petrol blower or vacuum

Petrol chainsaw

Reaching up

There is a limit to how high you can safely reach, especially if you are using power tools. Stepladders can be used for trimming tall hedges as long as the ground is even beneath their feet. They can tip over if you lean out too far, but they do not lean into and deform the plant you are pruning. Ladders can slip sideways and should always be used with care. With trees, the rule is always to face the ladder into the centre of the tree. For hedges, lean the ladder against the hedge. If the hedge is a bit thin, strap a plank of wood to the top of the ladder to stop it sinking in too far.

It is safer to use a tower scaffold of some description. These are stable and stand on four adjustable legs, and some have wheels so they can be moved around. However, they are bulky, can be cumbersome to move when erected, and you will need somewhere to store them. Hedge trimmers and chainsaws are now available on extension arms so that you don't have to climb.

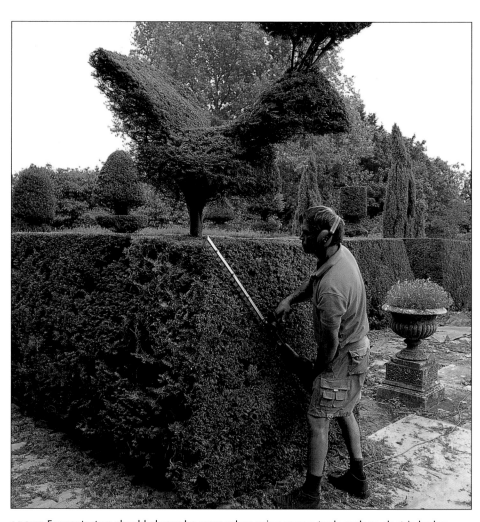

ABOVE Ear protectors should always be worn when using power tools such as electric hedge trimmers – but keep an eye out for anyone approaching you unheard.

ABOVE One or more legs can sink into the ground, toppling the step ladder, but special pads will prevent this.

ABOVE Special step ladders with a platform and a wide base make working on tall hedges both safer and easier.

Safety equipment

Observing safety precautions is very important if accidents are to be avoided. The operator should always be fully protected, with ear protectors, goggles, hard hats, gloves and boots with steel toecaps all being very important. A hard hat that also includes a face shield and ear protectors is a very good idea. Providing bystanders with safety equipment should not prove necessary, as they should be kept well out of harm's way at all times. When you are wearing ear protectors, someone may approach you undetected, so always keep a sharp eye out. If your hat takes a heavy knock from a branch, replace it, as the impact may have impaired its strength.

BASIC SAFETY EQUIPMENT

Unfortunately, accidents in the garden are very common and the availability of mechanized tools to the general gardener has added to the possible dangers. It is essential that proper safety gear, such as hard hats and goggles, is worn when you are carrying out certain pruning jobs. It is worth reiterating that certain jobs are best left to professional companies.

Ear protectors

Eye protectors

Safety helmet

Safety helmet with visor and ear protectors

Visor and ear protectors

Safety gloves

Reinforced safety gloves

Safety boots

Reinforced rubber safety boots

Basic pruning techniques

Although different shrubs and trees may need different pruning techniques, the physical process of making the cuts is usually the same. Cuts are generally made with secateurs (pruners), or long-handled pruners for thicker growth, or a saw of some kind.

Clean cuts

There are several general principles that apply when you are using all types of pruning equipment. The first may seem obvious, but it is often overlooked. The cut must be clean and there should be no tears in the wood or bits left hanging around the cut. The one essential requirement for achieving this, besides the ability to use the tools properly, is for the tools to be sharp and well maintained. A pair of secateurs that crushes the wood, rather than cleanly cutting through it, can cause problems.

When pruning trees, be aware that branches can be heavy, so avoid cutting straight through one in such a way that the weight makes it fall before you have finished cutting, tearing back along the branch or even down the trunk.

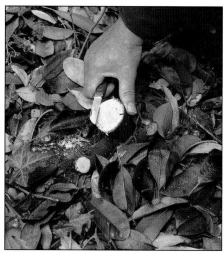

ABOVE After sawing through a thick stem, tidy up the cut by paring round the edge, creating a neat bevel.

Avoid snags

The second basic principle is to avoid snags. Snags are the short pieces of wood that stick out beyond a branch or a bud. All cuts should be made tight against the stem or up to a bud if removing the end of a shoot. Any piece of wood sticking out will not only look ugly but will usually die back, leaving dead wood through which diseases can enter. On roses, for example, if you leave a snag when deadheading, the stem may die back not just to the next bud but further down the branch.

ABOVE Secateurs are used for cutting thin shoots and branches. They should be sharp, so that the wood is cut cleanly and not bruised.

Ends of shoots or branches

When you are removing the end of a shoot or a branch, a sloping cut should be made just above the nearest bud to the point at which you want to shorten the shoot. The cut should be sloped at 45 degrees away from the bud (be careful not to cut through the bud). If you do accidentally cut through the bud, it may be necessary to recut back to the next bud. If there are two buds opposite one another, make the cut directly across the stem just above the pair of buds.

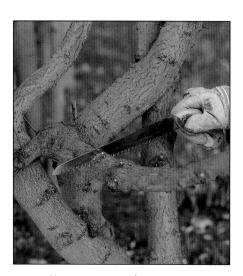

ABOVE Use a proper pruning saw to cut thicker branches. Avoid using carpenter's tools, which are not suitable for pruning.

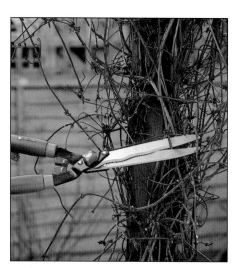

ABOVE Hedging shears are useful for cutting back large quantities of thin wood where the cuts do not have to be precise.

ABOVE Long-handled pruners are secateurs on long handles, and will cut through thicker wood.

ABOVE Most shears have a notch near the hinge, which is useful for cutting thicker wood when trimming hedges.

Removing a branch or stem

Always cut off a branch or heavier stem with three cuts. This will help prevent the branch splitting. The first cut is made some way out (about 30cm/12in or so) from the trunk, in an upward direction, about

THE PRUNING CUT
The perfect cut through a shoot or thin branch is a sloping one, angled just above and away from a bud.

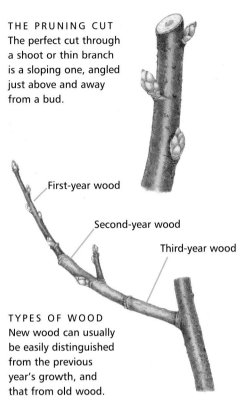

First-year wood

Second-year wood

Third-year wood

TYPES OF WOOD
New wood can usually be easily distinguished from the previous year's growth, and that from old wood.

a third of the way through. The second is made 8cm (3in) further along the branch and in a downward direction. As you pass the initial cut the branch will sag and split along to the second cut but will go no further. You can now cut straight through the remaining stub, close to the trunk.

Sealing wounds

Argument has raged for many years as to whether larger cuts should be sealed with some form of compound. Although some gardeners still stick to the practice, most now feel it is best to leave all cuts open to the air and weather. Trim round the cut with a sharp knife to remove any rough bark.

INCORRECT AND CORRECT PRUNING CUTS

Incorrect cut Do not make the cut too close to a bud. Aim to make the cut about a quarter of an inch above a bud.

Incorrect cut Do not cut too far above a bud, leaf or shoot because the remaining stub is likely to cause die-back.

Incorrect cut Do not slope the cut towards the bud as this is likely to cause rotting if water drains into it.

Incorrect cut All pruning cuts should be clean, with no bruising or ragged edges because these will allow disease to enter.

Correct cut The ideal cut is one that slants away, just above the bud. This will shed the rain away from the bud.

Correct cut When a pair of buds is involved, cut straight across the stem, just above the buds, without damaging either.

Ornamental Trees

Ornamental trees are among the easiest of woody plants to prune. Generally there is very little, if anything, to do. The only time there is real work is when they overgrow their allotted space or if they need repair work after a storm or high wind has blown off or damaged branches. Most of the work, and that rarely involves more than a few minutes, is in the initial stages, when the tree is first planted. It is important to ensure that the tree starts off growing the way you want it to.

The final shape is, of course, important. Most trees adopt their own shape but they may need a bit of initial help. For example, some trees develop a single, straight trunk, while others have multiple ones. *Amelanchier*, and some others, can have either, and this is where the training becomes important. Small weeping trees may also need a bit of special attention to ensure that they remain small and weeping. But even taking this into account, little work will be required, especially in small gardens where only one or two trees are involved.

LEFT An ornamental cherry tree in full flower, with an underplanting of daffodils. Cherries are usually easy to cope with because they need little pruning.

Buying young trees

As a general principle it is important to buy trees from a reputable supplier. It might cost a bit more but the quality should be good and many suppliers guarantee that if the plant fails within a certain period they will replace it.

What to look for

Always examine the tree thoroughly. Reject any trees that are diseased or are covered with some pest. Never buy a plant that is damaged. If the plant is pot-bound, i.e. the roots go round and round in a tight mass inside the pot, again reject it. Bare-root plants should not be desiccated and the roots should not be damaged.

Look for a plant that has a well-balanced structure and a healthy appearance. Avoid buying trees that have too much growth on them as these can be slow to establish. There is a balance between the amount of root and the amount of top growth it can support. In a nursery, trees have been intensively nurtured. Once planted out they have to fend for

ABOVE The most common way to acquire new trees is through nursery-produced stock that is sold in containers.

themselves to a certain extent and too much top growth during the initial stages will cause problems.

Most trees offered for sale will be one or more years old. The older, the more expensive, but they should be at least partially trained. Such a tree will not be too difficult to establish. A one-year-old is cheaper and easy to establish but takes longer to mature, but at least you can be in full control of its development and shape.

Be careful how you get your tree home. Damage can easily occur if you have a tall sapling sticking out of your sunroof, or if it is carelessly handled. Keep the tree in a cool spot prior to planting and water it well to make sure it does not dry out. Occasionally you may acquire a tree in a bare-rooted state. This is most likely to be as a gift from a friend as increasingly nursery-sold plants are in pots. Such trees should be put in the ground as soon as possible, even if it is only in a temporary position.

It is, of course, possible to grow your own trees from seed, cuttings, grafts or even divisions in some

cases. This will obviously take much longer than buying an established tree but there is a certain satisfaction in growing your own plants from scratch. Besides being cheaper, you also have the possibility of controlling the whole process to get what you really want.

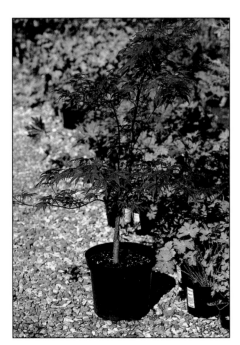

ABOVE When buying trees and shrubs in containers, make certain that the roots have not become too congested within the pot.

ABOVE In general, trees can be grown on as they are, but occasionally they have wayward branches that need trimming.

Feathered trees

Virtually any single-stemmed tree can be feathered. Some feathered trees have a clearly defined shape, whereas others tend to have a more wayward appearance, which is part of their charm. As an extreme example, oak trees (*Quercus*) can have a very regular upright appearance or they can be allowed to grow with a twisted, irregular silhouette. Conifers are perhaps the most obvious example of feathered trees, with their almost pure cone-shapes.

Planting

Plant the tree in well-prepared soil with its roots spread out and not wound round or crammed into the hole. Do not prune the roots unless they are damaged, in which case just remove the damaged parts. The tree should be supported by a short stake that is inserted before the tree is put

ABOVE Conifers very rarely need much pruning. They look better if allowed to take on their natural shape.

TRAINING A FEATHERED TREE

Choose either a maiden whip or a young feathered tree that has an even structure and an intact leader. The leader is important if you want your tree to have a straight trunk. It is possible to train a replacement leader on some trees.

YEAR ONE On planting, remove any dead or wayward branches, especially those that cross or rub against others.

YEAR TWO In general, very little pruning is required other than keeping the shape balanced and the trunk clear.

into the ground. This ensures that you do not accidentally damage unseen roots when you hammer the stake into the soil.

Formative pruning

The aim is to produce a healthy, well-shaped tree. First remove any dead branches or any that have been damaged during transportation or planting. This will help maintain the plant's health. The next task (which is partly cosmetic and partly to do with health) is to remove branches that cross or rub against each other or grow at too sharp an angle to the trunk. This not only improves the tree's appearance but also ensures that no wounds open up. Any other badly placed branches can also be

removed, especially round the base of the plant. It is best in most trees (except conifers) to have a clean, visible length of trunk, even if it is only short. The tree should now be straight with well-spaced, healthy branches.

Next year, repeat the above process. Be careful to remove any vigorous upright shoots that have developed, as these can compete with the leader, either to give the tree a split head or turn it into a multi-stemmed one.

Trees suitable for feathering

Lawson cypress	Larch (*Larix*)
(*Chamaecyparis*	Spruce (*Picea*)
lawsoniana)	Thuya (*Thuja*)

Standard trees

Any tree that grows with a bare lower trunk is suitable for training into a standard. Training may even be unnecessary because some trees will develop this habit naturally.

Training a standard tree

These are essentially the same as feathered trees except that more of the lower branches are removed so that the lower part of the trunk can be clearly seen. Although the term "standard" usually refers to a tree with a clear trunk, it is also often used to refer to a tree that has grown to a natural shape and size rather than one that has been dwarfed in some way.

The shape is perhaps not quite as "pure" as in the case of a feathered tree. Feathered trees normally have only one central leader, whereas a standard may have one or it may divide at some point on the trunk and have several. The degree of natural division often depends on

HOW TO TRAIN A STANDARD BIRCH TREE

1 (*left*) Most birch trees develop a natural shape and there is not much pruning required to keep them looking their best.

2 (*above*) However, if there are any wayward branches, as at the bottom of this particular tree, then they should be cleanly removed.

the situation in which the tree is being grown. For example, an oak tree growing among other trees will often grow tall and slender with just the one leader, but in isolation it will branch out and have a much more rounded shape. In the garden, the leader can be allowed to develop, giving a tall elegant tree, or it can be cut back to produce a branched-head standard, which has a rounder shape. In many cases the tree will

TRAINING A SINGLE-STEMMED STANDARD

Tall trees that have a single stem can look slim and elegant in the garden. It is essential that the central leader grows without being pruned or broken. If it does break, a new leader must be trained in its place if this is possible.

YEAR ONE Remove some of the lowest side shoots to partially clear the trunk, and cut back by a half those that will be removed next year.

YEAR TWO ONWARDS Follow the same procedure as for the previous year until the lowest branches are reached and take out any crossed-over shoots.

TRAINING A BRANCH-HEADED STANDARD

Branch-headed standards are rounder and have a more solid appearance than single-stemmed standards. Here, the leader is removed, as are any branches that attempt to replace it, creating a good framework of branches.

YEAR ONE The procedure is the same as for a single-leader standard except that the leader is taken out where the topmost branch reaches the trunk.

YEAR TWO ONWARDS Continue to remove the lower side-shoots until the bottom branch is reached, and take out any misplaced shoots.

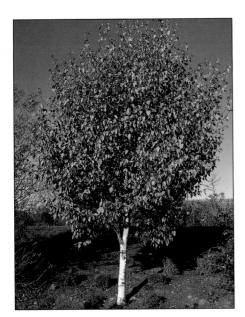

ABOVE The well-cleared trunk of this beautiful birch tree draws attention to the distinctive silvery bark for which it is valued.

Trees suitable for training as standards

Maple (*Acer*)	Tulip tree
Chestnut	(*Liriodendron*)
(*Aesculus*)	Crab apple (*Malus*)
Alder (*Alnus*)	Pine (*Pinus*)
Birch (*Betula*)	Poplar (*Populus*)
Hornbeam	Cherry (*Prunus*)
(*Carpinus*)	Almond
Indian bean tree	(*Prunus dulcis*)
(*Catalpa*)	Pear (*Pyrus*)
Ash (*Fraxinus*)	Oak (*Quercus*)
Laburnum	Willow (*Salix*)
(*Laburnum*)	Rowan (*Sorbus*)
	Lime (*Tilia*)

PRUNING A WEEPING STANDARD
Keep the trunks of weeping standards clear of shoots, and remove any shoots that spoil the shape by not weeping nicely.

automatically try to replace this lost leader. In such a case, the gardener will need to be vigilant and prune each new leader out to maintain the desired shape. Conversely, developing a tree with a single leader requires training one main shoot, while others are restrained.

Training a weeping standard

Weeping trees are highly regarded as ornamental plants in the garden. There are basically two types of weeping standard. One comprises trees such as the weeping willow, which have a natural weeping shape. The other type is artificially created.

Ground-spreading plants are grafted on to a standard trunk some distance from the ground so that they spread into the air rather than across the soil, often, when bare, creating a shape like the ribs of an open umbrella.

The natural weeping trees are essentially treated in the same way as standard trees. Pruning can be restricted to removing any dead, injured, weak or crossing wood.

The grafted weepers may need a bit more attention. Unlike the natural weeping trees, which need to put on upward growth in order to obtain their tree-like shape, the grafted varieties need to have any vertical shoots removed. At the same

time, any new growth on the trunk below the canopy should be removed. They also have a tendency to become somewhat tangled and congested, so remove crossing or weak growth. As all the growth is concentrated in the canopy while the trunk remains relatively thin, it is obviously important to make sure at this stage that the tree is well supported with a strong stake.

ABOVE This weeping standard is becoming too thick and some of the branches will need to be thinned out.

Trees suitable for training as weeping standards

Weeping maple (*Acer palmatum* 'Jiro-shodare')

Weeping alder (*Alnus incana* 'Pendula')

Weeping birch (*Betula pendula*)

Weeping hornbeam (*Carpinus betulus* 'Pendula')

Weeping ash (*Fraxinus sylvatica* 'Pendula')

Weeping holly (*Ilex aquifolium* 'Argentea Pendula')

Weeping laburnum (*Laburnum alpinum* 'Pendulum')

Weeping ornamental cherries (*Prunus* cvs)

Weeping pear (*Pyrus salicifolia* 'Pendula')

Weeping willow (*Salix babylonica*; *S. caprea* 'Kilmarnock'; *S. × chrysocoma*; *S. matsudana* 'Pendula'; *S. purpurea* 'Pendula')

Weeping sorbus (*Sorbus aucuparia* 'Pendula')

Multi-stemmed trees

Some trees naturally form multiple trunks (although some gardeners would argue that a tree with multiple trunks is a shrub). In many, if not most cases, trees with multiple stems can also develop as more conventional trees with a single trunk that divides some way above the ground. *Amelanchier* is a good example. The multiple stems may be natural or artificially produced, both in the wild and in the garden. Any feathered tree that is broken off, by accident or design, just above ground level will probably produce multiple stems. There are also trees, such as plum, that produce suckers, and these by their very nature produce more than one main stem.

Formative pruning

The initial pruning is relatively simple. If you have bought a young single-stemmed tree, you have to bite the bullet and throw most of it away! Cut through the main stem just above ground level, or at whatever height you want the

TRAINING A MULTI-STEMMED TREE

Multi-stemmed trees tend to look rather like overgrown shrubs. Indeed, they are often regarded by gardeners as shrubs rather than trees. They can vary from having just two or three stems to what amounts to a thicket.

YEAR ONE Cut through the trunk of a suitable feathered tree at the height at which you want the multiple stems to start.

YEAR TWO After a year, select the most suitable stems in order to create a balanced tree and remove the rest.

YEAR THREE Continue to train the individual main stems by removing any dead wood or any branches that cross or rub against each other.

division of the trunk to begin. Once new growth appears from the base, select the required number (three or more) of shoots and remove the others. This will form the basis of your tree, so select the strongest growing shoots, which will make a balanced tree. Continue to train these as you would a tree with a single stem, removing diseased, dead, weak or crossing growth.

Not all trees will shoot from the base after such drastic action, but a surprising number will. However, you should be selective, as not all trees look best with multiple stems.

ABOVE This *Acer palmatum*, bursting into leaf, shows very clearly the beauty of its multiple stems.

Trees suitable for training with multiple stems

Maple (*Acer*)
Alder (*Alnus*)
Serviceberry (*Amelanchier*)
Strawberry tree (*Arbutus*)
Hornbeam (*Carpinus*)
Judas tree (*Cercis*)
Magnolia (*Magnolia*)
Sumach (*Rhus*)
Sweet chestnut (*Castanea*)
Willow (*Salix*)
Wingnut (*Pterocarya*)

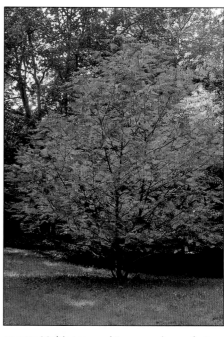

ABOVE Multi-stemmed trees can be perfect for the larger garden. This is the rare but beautiful *Pterocarya stenoptera*.

Young evergreens

The initial training of an evergreen tree is not a great deal different to that of deciduous trees.

Training young evergreens

Conifers are generally dealt with as if they were feathered trees. In other words, only dead, injured or diseased wood is removed, along with any badly placed shoots or a competitive leader. Generally they are developed so that they are clothed with branches to the ground, but the bottom ones can be removed to leave a bare trunk, as with standard trees. Many conifers naturally make a beautiful cone shape, or, as in the case of some pines, their own distinct shape. Some are naturally weeping.

Broadleaved evergreens such as hollies (*Ilex*) are also pruned in similar fashion although they can, in many cases, be more drastically cut and turned into multi-stemmed trees, either dividing at ground-level or at any height above it. They are more suitable for shaping than conifers, giving you the chance, for example, of creating a tree with a wide crown to cover an eyesore. Evergreens are generally much denser than deciduous trees and throw a

deep shade as opposed to a dappled one. For even denser growth it is possible to shorten the side shoots to make them bush out.

Evergreens suitable for training

Conifers (most)
Winter's bark (*Drimys winteri*)
Eucalyptus (*Eucalyptus*)
Eucryphia (*Eucryphia*)
Hoheria (*Hoheria angustifolia*)
Holly (*Ilex*)
Magnolia (*Magnolia grandiflora*)
Holm oak (*Quercus ilex*)

TRAINING A YOUNG EVERGREEN

It is possible to train evergreen trees into a variety of different shapes in the same way as you would train deciduous trees. However, most conifers are trained as single-stemmed standards.

YEAR ONE Very little pruning is required, although the bottom branches need removing if you want a bare trunk.

SUBSEQUENT YEARS Apart from the removal of any crossing or dead branches, there is again very little pruning required.

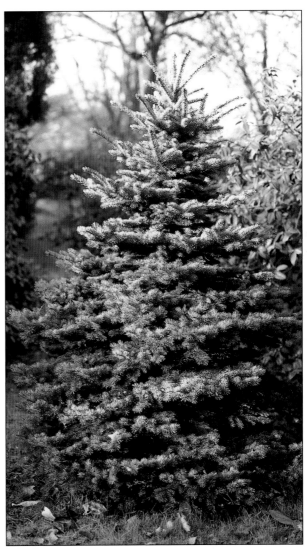

ABOVE Young conifers rarely need any training, and look better if clothed to the ground with branches.

Established pruning

With proper initial training most trees are set up for life and apart from a regular check-up rarely need much attention. It is possible to ignore their pruning totally and the tree will still thrive, much as they all do in the wild. However, a healthy tree is a far safer one as well as a prettier one, and so it is worth spending a short while each year checking any trees over.

The three Ds

The one gardening task that must be carried out at least once a year is a survey of all the trees in the garden in order to check that there is no dead, diseased or damaged wood. Any that is found should be cut out and the wounds cleaned up. It is probably a good idea to check at the end of the growing season, in autumn, and again after the winter during which strong winds and frost may have caused damage to your trees.

ABOVE Unusual trees, such as this weeping cherry, need special attention or they will lose the quality that makes them such an attractive feature in the garden.

Fallen branches should have the snags cut off and any tears should be cleaned with a sharp knife to remove all fragments of loose wood. Any heavy branches that are to be removed should be cut off in sections to prevent splitting and tearing. There is no need to dress wounds even from cuts left by the removal of large branches.

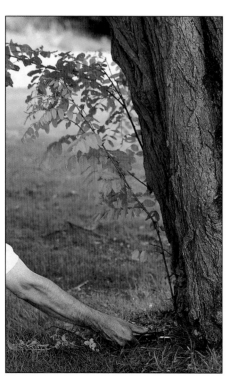

ABOVE Many trees produce suckers from the base of the trunk. These should be cut out as tightly to the trunk as possible.

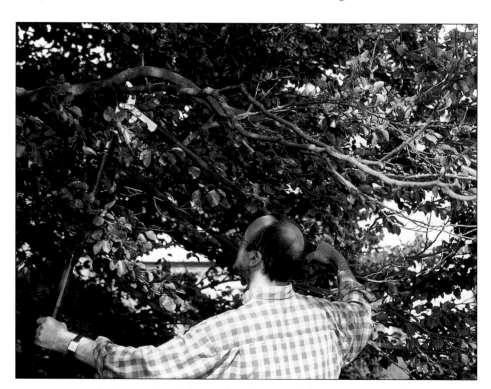

ABOVE It is essential that any dead, damaged or dying wood should be removed from your trees. Autumn and winter storms can be a cause of damage that will need dealing with in the spring. Here, a pair of long-handled pruners is being used to remove a dead branch.

ABOVE Clean any larger cuts with a sharp knife to remove any ragged or torn bark.

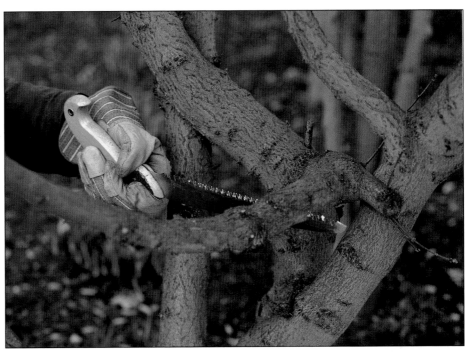

ABOVE Usually little pruning is required for trees, but it is likely to help if any crossing or over-crowding branches are removed.

Unwanted growths

Most trees at some point produce branches that cross others, creating congestion and often wounds where the bark of one rubs against that of

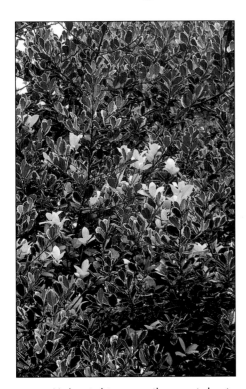

ABOVE Variegated trees can throw out shoots on which the leaves revert to their original green. Remove these when you see them.

another in the wind. Any such crossing wood should be removed. If you are creating a branch-headed standard then it is also a good idea to thin the timber in the centre of the tree so that air and light can circulate.

Many trees from time to time throw out wayward growths – an odd stem will suddenly shoot off into space – spoiling the shape of the plant. These should be removed at some point within the shape of the

tree. Similarly, if the tree is a variety with variegation or non-standard foliage, it may occasionally throw out reverted stems, with leaves that are plain green, like those of the parent species. These should be removed back at their point of origin.

Some trees produce water (or epicormic) shoots. These are shoots that appear around wounds where, for example, a branch has been removed or where a lawn mower has

DEALING WITH EPICORMIC SHOOTS

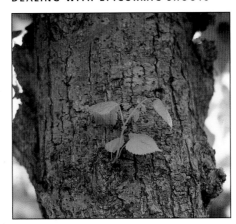

1 Some trees – lime (*Tilia*) in particular – produce what are known as water or epicormic shoots on their trunks.

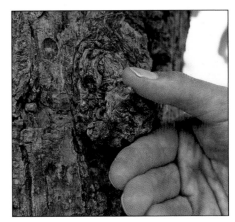

2 The best way of dealing with them is to rub them out with your fingers as soon as you see them.

REMOVING A LARGE TREE BRANCH

1 Make a cut about 20–25cm (8–10in) out from where the final cut will be on the underside of the branch. Cut about a third of the way into the branch.

2 Make a cut about 10cm (4in) nearer the position of the final cut, cutting until the branch snaps. The initial undercut prevents the wood splitting or bark from stripping.

3 Position the saw for the last cut to avoid damaging the swollen area at the base of the branch. The cut will heal in a couple of seasons. No wound painting is necessary.

damaged the bark at the base of the trunk. Cut these out at their base. If the tree has been grafted, then any shoots that appear from below the graft union should be removed, even if they look as though they might be in the ideal place, as these will be different from the rest of the tree. Similarly, suckers often appear from below ground. These may come from a grafted rootstock or just as a natural suckering habit. Unless you want to develop a multi-stemmed tree, these should all be removed back at their point of origin. Dig below soil level, if necessary.

Controlling size

In an ideal world it would be nice to allow trees to grow to their full potential, but there are often factors, such as a lack of space, which dictate that the tree should be kept to a certain size. In some cases this may simply be a question of removing a few side branches, perhaps even spoiling the shape. In other cases, it may mean reducing the size of the whole tree. One technique is known as dropcrotching: all the branches are reduced in length, so that the original outline of the tree is kept the same but much reduced in size. This should be done before the tree reaches its ultimate size, while the branches are still quite young, so that the shaping will not be too unsightly. Repeat every two or three years. Do not cut too deeply back into the tree or it may never recover its shape.

Letting in light

It has already been mentioned that it can sometimes be beneficial to open up the canopy to let in more light and air, particularly with fruiting trees. In addition, you may wish to grow other plants below trees, and too dense a shade will often prevent this. In order to let in more light (and, indeed, water in the form of rain), rather than remove the whole tree it

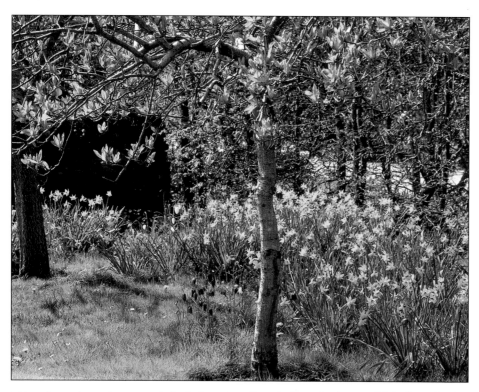

ABOVE In gardens where space is limited or where there is close planting, established pruning is required to control the size of a tree and so prevent it from smothering other plants.

ABOVE Working with ladders can be dangerous for those not used to them. This stepladder with a wide base is a much safer option.

is often possible to remove some of the lower branches. This is often done with oak trees, the shape of which is not unduly spoilt by such pruning. It allows grass and other plants to be grown beneath them.

Feeling their age

As with humans, trees age. In oaks, this may well be only after several hundred years, but it might be only after 30 in the case of birches. There are several problems associated with this. One is the development of stags' heads. This is most noticeable in oaks but can also occur in other trees. Some of the branches die, leaving them bare and stripped of bark (often looking like a stag's horns, hence the name). In some cases this makes the tree look venerable, but others will simply look diseased and unsightly. The tree is usually perfectly healthy, and the removal of the branches will return the tree to its normal appearance.

The other problem is that branches may start to sag and fall away. A similar and more frequent occurrence is when the trunks of multi-stemmed trees start to fall apart. These can be braced if the tree is an important one. This is best done by experienced professionals, as an inadequately braced tree may fall on somebody with dire consequences all round.

Safety

Ladder work may be necessary when pruning tall trees. If you do not feel confident or have not had the necessary experience of cutting large branches from a tree, especially those that are some way from the ground, call in a tree expert. It may cost money but not lives. If you do the work yourself, wear adequate safety gear, especially a hard hat.

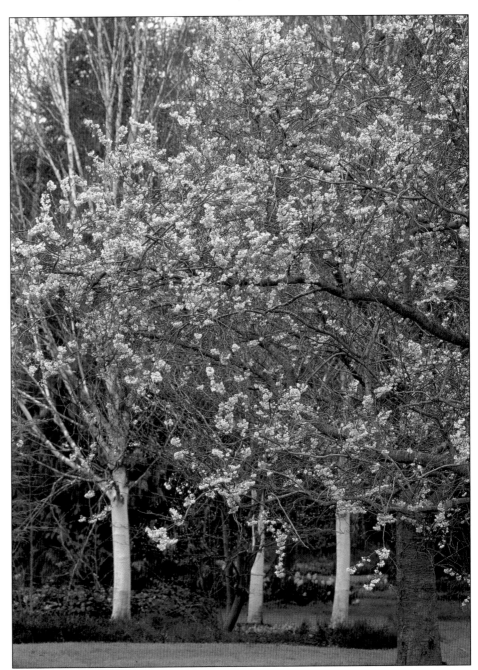

ABOVE Most fully grown trees, such as these ornamental cherries (*Prunus*) or the birches (*Betula*) in the background, need little in the way of pruning.

Renovation pruning

When you take over an old garden, or acquire a new one which was part of a field or wood, there may be old trees in it that have been neglected or never been pruned. You may well be forced to decide whether to take the trees out and start from scratch, or try to renovate them. Trees take a long time to grow to maturity and leave a large gap when felled, so if possible it is best to try to bring them back to their former glory. There may also be preservation orders on the trees, so it would be illegal to remove them without permission. It may even be illegal to carry out major renovation without permission, so it is always best to check before you start.

Prune it step by step

Your aim with a neglected and overgrown tree is to turn back the clock and do all the things that should have been carried out in previous years. The best time to rejuvenate an old tree is in the late autumn or early winter. Start, as always, by removing any dead, diseased or damaged wood. This should remove quite a bit of material and allow you to begin to see the structure of the tree. Next remove any water or epicormic shoots along with any weak growths, especially those that have developed in the centre of the tree. Where branches cross over or rub against other branches, cut them out. The tree should now begin to look the way it should.

Examine the tree closely to assess whether there is still any overcrowding and whether anything else needs to be removed. Perhaps the tree has been regularly "pruned" by somebody who has simply gone over the outside of the tree

1 (*left*) Some trees, such as this contorted hazel, can become overgrown and need to be renovated in order to bring back their shape and interest.

2 (*above*) Start the renovation by removing all the dead and damaged wood. This will allow you to see what remains much more clearly.

3 (*left*) Next thin some of the branches to reduce the congestion, especially towards the middle of the tree. Remove old and weak growths first.

4 (*above*) The dead stub shows how poor pruning can cause die-back, as the previous cut was made too high. Cut tightly back as shown here.

PRUNING KNOBBLY SPURS If a tree has been severely cut back over a number of years, the ends of the branches become a mass of spurs. Cut these back drastically to one or two in order to return the tree to its original shape.

Tree renovation times

Mid- to late winter (before growth starts)
Birch (*Betula*)
Conifers
Horse chestnut (*Aesculus*)
Maple (*Acer*)
Walnut (*Juglans*)
Willow (*Salix*)

Any season apart from spring
Beech (*Fagus*)
Hornbeam) *Carpinus*
Lime (*Tilia*)
Oak (*Quercus*)

Summer (before end of mid-summer)
Ornamental plums and cherries

TREE RENOVATION TECHNIQUES

In general, most ornamental trees can be left to their own devices, but sometimes it is essential to remove the lower branches or thin the crown in order to allow more light and rain to reach any plants that are growing under the tree.

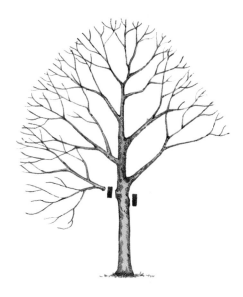

CROWN RAISING More light can be obtained below a tree by removing some of the lower branches so that the light comes in under the canopy.

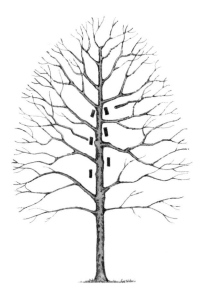

CROWN THINNING An alternative method is to thin out some of the branches from the crown so that dappled light filters its way through the canopy.

removing the new extension growth on the tips of the branches, so that it has thickened up around the perimeter, a bit like a hedge. You will have to reduce and thin this growth drastically to bring the tree back to something resembling a normal appearance.

Not all trees like to be pruned hard all in one go, as it can often kill them. It is usually better to prune them over a number of years, taking out just a bit each time. This means that the tree will look untidy over this period, but this is better than a dead tree.

Aftercare

Renovation is a drastic treatment for any tree, so make certain that it is fed and kept watered during any dry spells the following summer. Mulching will help to preserve soil moisture.

Safety

A lot of the pruning work on an overgrown tree inevitably takes place well above the head of the gardener, usually on ladders. If you do not feel confident to carry out this work yourself, then employ a specialist firm who will have had a lot of experience in dealing with this kind of renovation work. This is particularly important if you need, for example, to take out a dead crown from a large tree.

ABOVE Overgrown trees will inevitably contain a lot of dead and damaged wood. This should be one of the first things to be removed.

ABOVE If a tree has been neglected, there are likely to be branches that cross over or rub against others. These should be removed.

Pruning conifers

Conifers are very popular trees and shrubs, forming an architectural backbone to the garden that varies only slightly from season to season. They are also relatively easy to grow and require little attention once they have been planted. Unfortunately, many gardeners do not realize that they must be treated differently from their deciduous relatives. How often do you see a row of dead coniferous trees where the owner has decided that they have grown too large and so has lopped off half of each tree, only to discover that it was the wrong thing to do?

Cutting into old wood

Most conifers are very reluctant to put out new shoots from old wood, so cut back only into the new growth. Cutting back into the older wood creates a bald patch, and removing too much can result in the death of the tree. If you want to control the height, either ensure in the first place that the tree you buy will reach only the height you want it to, or be prepared to treat it like a hedge and clip it regularly once or twice a year, removing only some of the new growth.

What to prune

Having placed restrictions on pruning of conifers, there are still

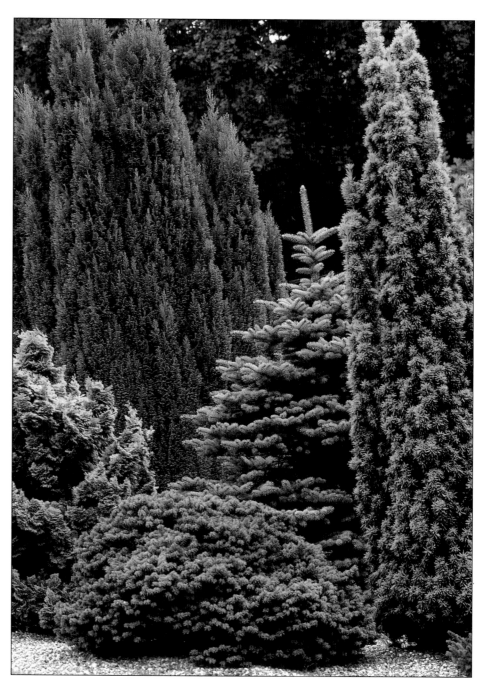

ABOVE Many garden conifers have a beautiful natural shape and, given enough space in which to grow, require very little pruning.

ABOVE One task that always needs doing is the removal of dead branches. Cut back to good wood. Growth will spread to fill the gap.

tasks that need to be carried out. As always, any dead, dying, damaged or diseased wood should be cut out, preferably as far back as possible. Also remove any odd growths that stick out beyond the required shape. Do not leave these for too long or they may grow too vigorously and leave a hole when you remove them. Similarly, on variegated conifers, there may be some reversion

(plain green leaves), and this needs to be removed or it will gradually dominate to the detriment of the variegation. As we have already mentioned, a light clipping to keep the size and shape is generally the best strategy, but this is really only necessary with trees where the shape is very important, such as with pure cone shapes or slim columnar trees.

Pruning conifers

Most conifers will stand a little light pruning as long as you restrict yourself to the new growth. In general, this will apply only if you are cutting the tree to a shape, as in topiary, or creating a hedge. If done every year, this will also help to restrict its size. However, once a conifer has reached maturity, there is little that can be done to reduce its size except in the following examples. These will tolerate being cut back into old wood. One of the most common garden conifers, the Lawson cypress, *Chamaecyparis lawsoniana*, will not break from old wood, so do not attempt to prune it except for a light trim to retain size and shape.

Cephalotaxus	*Sequoia*
Cryptomeria	*Taxus*
Cunninghamia	*Torreya*

Tying in

As trees get old and large, snow and sometimes wind can pull a branch out of place so that it sticks out sideways. This is a problem with shaped trees that have several main stems or near-vertical branches. If removed, these will leave a large gap that is unlikely to be refilled with new shoots. The

PRUNING TECHNIQUES FOR CONIFERS

1 If it is necessary to prune conifers, cut the shoots well back into the tree, so that their removal does not show.

2 Dead wood will always spoil the appearance of a conifer and should be removed as soon as possible.

3 Conifers do not need much pruning, but new growth can be clipped over to restrict the size of the tree. Do not cut into old wood.

4 Rather than shear over the tree and cut some leaves in half, it is neater to pinch out the growing tips to restrict growth.

only solution is to pull them back into position and tie them in place. Protect the bark with wadding (batting) so that the wire or rope does not chafe. If large branches are involved, you may need professional help.

If the tree is hopelessly distorted, it is often advisable to start again with a new tree. A conifer in such a poor state is very difficult to renovate and can look distinctly ugly if left as it is.

REMOVING A COMPETING LEADER

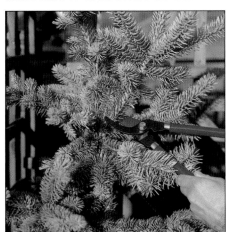

1 If a young conifer has two competing leaders, one of them should be removed to restore its single-stemmed shape.

2 If the new leader is not growing strongly upright, tie a cane to the main stem. Tie the leader to the cane to encourage vertical growth.

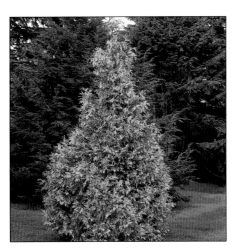

ABOVE Some conifers take on a regular shape, and these may need occasional pruning to keep the outline.

Felling trees

There are some tasks that most gardeners will only occasionally come across and perhaps never at all. The main one is the felling of a tree. This is not an easy task at the best of times, but toppling a large tree in a small garden without damaging anything in the process is very tricky indeed.

Can you do it?

Felling trees is really a job for the professional. Even if the way is clear, if the tree is by a lawn for example, it is still a skilled job to get it to drop exactly where required. If it is growing among other trees or shrubs, or stands near fences or buildings, it can be more of a problem. Such trees usually need to be taken down branch by branch, which involves quite a lot of clambering around in the tree. Apart from all the skills that this requires there is also the question of equipment. Not many gardeners have chainsaws capable of dealing with a tree and although you can hire them, they are dangerous

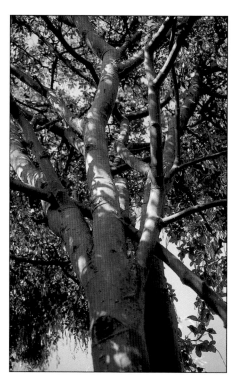

ABOVE One tree has fallen into another and it will be a tricky job, involving climbing into the tree, to get it down safely.

tools to use. They should be employed only if you have taken a course in their use and safety.

Professional tree surgeons do this kind of work all the time and, if they

are a good team, will know precisely how to get the tree down without damaging property or themselves. They will also be insured in case anything goes wrong.

Employing tree surgeons

Always ensure that you are employing people who have been properly trained and belong to a professional association. Check that they are fully insured. If you have no need for the wood or have not got the facilities for its disposal, make certain that they will remove it. Nowadays they will often mechanically shred the brushwood and this is worth keeping and composting to use as a mulch.

Shy away from anyone knocking on the door and offering to take the tree down. It may seem a bargain at first, but such people are rarely skilled enough to do the job properly and if anything goes wrong you could be faced with a very large compensation bill because they are bound not to be insured.

ABOVE This is not the kind of job for the average gardener; a skilled professional who knows what he is doing is required for this work.

ABOVE Removing tall trees in a restricted space without causing damage is highly skilled and must be left to the professionals.

FELLING A SMALL TREE

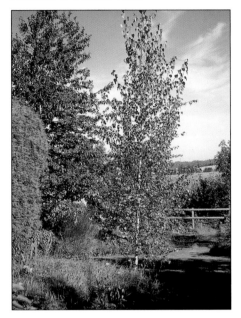

1 Small trees, such as this birch, that are situated in a clear space may well be within the capabilities of most gardeners, but do not tackle this job if you are in any doubt.

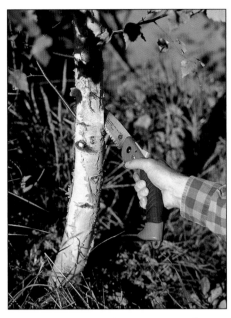

2 Start by making a sloping cut at 45 degrees on the side of the tree that is facing the direction in which you want it to fall. Go into the tree by between a quarter and one-third.

3 Follow this initial cut with a horizontal cut just below it, so that the two cuts eventually meet and you are able to remove a wedge of the trunk.

4 Remove the wedge from the trunk. This should ensure that when the tree is cut through, it will fall in the direction that you want it to.

5 Start sawing on the other side of the tree opposite the horizontal cut. As the saw nears the removed wedge of wood, the tree will fall forward.

6 Step back smartly as the tree falls, just in case it springs back as it hits the ground. Now you simply need to remove the stump from the ground.

What can you tackle?

If you are experienced in this area you can at least deal with small trees, especially multi-stemmed ones that are not too tall and heavy. But do not undertake this work unless you are confident of your abilities.

Before cutting, ensure that the ground is clear and that you can get away if anything goes wrong. For a clear fell, cut a notch on the side in the direction you want the tree to fall and then cut through from the other side level with this notch. The tree will start to topple in the right direction just before the trunk is cut through. Once it is down, dig up the remaining stump.

Before starting to fell, make certain that you can move back without tripping over and that the tree will not hit anything that can deflect it, and so land somewhere you did not want it too. Trees are large objects when on the ground, so ensure you have enough space.

Coppicing and pollarding

These two traditional techniques have generally dropped out of use both in the countryside and in gardens. Valuable both economically and aesthetically, they provided an important source of material for basket-weaving and fence-making, and enabled the growth of larger trees in a small space as well as producing good foliage.

Principles

Coppicing is the cutting back almost to ground level of all the main shoots of a multi-stemmed tree. These then regenerate and another set of main shoots develops, only for these to be removed as well. The wood may be thin and wispy, as in the case of willow, which is coppiced each year for weaving material, or quite thick and tall, as in sweet chestnut (*Castanea*), which is coppiced for poles on a cycle of up to 14 years.

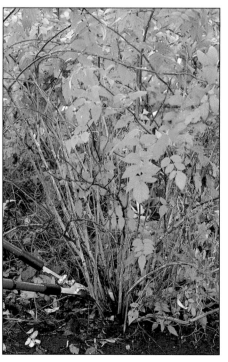

ABOVE Willows growing next to water are frequently coppiced or pollarded in order to provide material for basket-making and garden use.

Trees suitable for coppicing and pollarding

Ailanthus (*Ailanthus*)
Alder (*Alnus*)
Ash (*Fraxinus*)
Elder (*Sambucus*)Hazel (*Corylus*)
Eucalyptus (*Eucalyptus*)
Hazel *(Corylus)*
Hornbeam (*Carpinus*)
Indian bean tree (*Catalpa*)
Oak (*Quercus*)
Paulownia (*Paulownia*)
Sweet chestnut (*Castanea*)
Willow (*Salix*)

Pollarding is exactly the same except the cutting takes place at some height above the ground. Historically, this was done so that animals could not reach the new shoots. Again, the pollarding is done every year for thinner wood but at longer intervals for thicker material. Oak trees were pollarded so that the timber could be used for construction and firewood.

Modern uses

In the modern garden, the technique can still be used for the same purposes, particularly on willow to provide plant supports and other garden structures. It can also be

HOW TO COPPICE

1 Many plants with decorative stems in winter, such as this *Rubus*, should be coppiced in spring, before or just as they come into leaf.

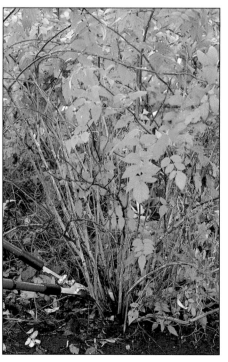

2 Cut out all the stems close to the ground. Some of the more shrubby plants need to be cut just above the previous year's cut.

3 Make all the cuts clean and slightly angled to allow rain to run off. Take this opportunity to remove any weeds growing in the centre.

POLLARDING A LARGE TREE

1 This specimen is typical of a tree that has been regularly pollarded. All the branches are rising from the top of the trunk, rather like unruly hair.

2 Remove all the branches, using either a pair of strong long-handled pruners or a saw. At this stage it does not matter if some of the stubs are rather long.

3 Tidy up the pruned cuts by sawing through the base of each of the branches The new shoots will eventually appear round the edge of these cuts.

used on hazel in order to provide sticks to support peas as well as herbaceous and annual plants. Some trees, such as elder (*Sambucus*) or eucalyptus, also respond by

producing large or attractive colourful foliage if they are regularly coppiced. It can also be used to reduce the size of trees, for example to restrict the growth of an Indian bean tree (*Catalpa*).

should subsequently be pollarded every one to three years in late winter by removing the shoots back to almost 1cm (½in) from the trunk.

Techniques

For coppicing, grow the tree as a multi-stemmed form. Once the poles have reached the required size, cut them off near the base with a saw in late winter to early spring. The cuts should be slightly sloped to allow rainwater to run off. Trim the bark neatly round the edge of the cut.

For pollarding, choose a tree with a main stem and plenty of side branches. Once it has become established, cut through the trunk above the group of shoots at the height at which you wish to form the head. Remove all other shoots below the main cluster. The trees

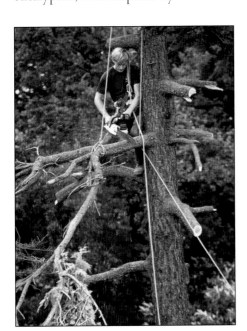

ABOVE Removing branches before felling a tree is akin to pollarding, and anything of this size must be tackled by a professional.

ABOVE Coloured winter stems are achieved by coppicing every year. It takes only a short while for the tree to recover.

Pleaching

Pleaching is a highly decorative form of pruning. It essentially produces a row of trees in which the branches are interlocked in a horizontal plane above a certain length of bare trunk, in effect making an elevated hedge. There are several variations on this. In some versions, parallel hedges are also trained across to form a horizontal or domed roof, while in others there is not only a roof but also ends, creating a room. In some versions, the side walls come right to the ground, although it is more normal to have them on stilts, as it were. In many areas of Europe, the trees are pleached just to produce a thin, horizontal roof, which protects the town squares from the glaring sun.

Principles

The aim is to train the branches horizontally along wires or battens until they meet and intermingle with those of their neighbours. Side shoots from these main branches are kept to a minimum, just enough to clothe the structure with leaves. Once established, pleached trees are no more difficult to maintain than a hedge, although they do need cutting from a ladder.

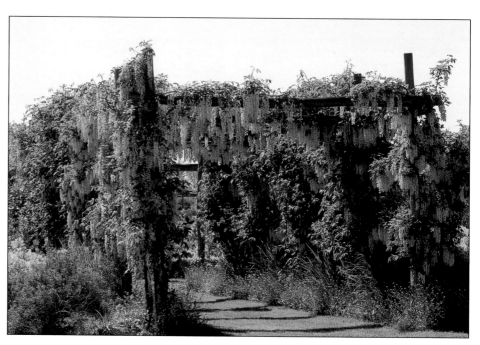

ABOVE Very attractive walkways can be achieved by pleaching trees, as this large pergola supporting a laburnum in full flower demonstrates.

Structure

The initial structure consists of stout vertical poles between which are stretched horizontal wires or wooden lathes. The verticals should be at about 2.5m (8ft) intervals, but this is only a rough guide as it is best to divide up the given space equally rather than have an odd distance somewhere in the line. The two end poles can be at the same distance as the others or can be reduced to half the distance from their neighbours. Fasten the battens or wires at 60cm (2ft) intervals. If you use wires, make certain that they are taut. Using tensioning screws or bolts that can be tightened as the wire stretches is a good idea.

ABOVE These pleached trees shown in winter reveal how they create both the sides and roof of a covered walkway that has now been filled with shrubs.

Trees suitable for pleaching

Beech (*Fagus*)
Holly (*Ilex*)
Hornbeam (*Carpinus*)
Laburnum
Lime (*Tilia*)* Possibly the most popular

Formative pruning

Plant trees at each of the posts, except the first and the last. These should be three- or four-year-old trees with a good structure of side shoots, the lowest being roughly level with the bottom wire. The general principle is to train the leader vertically until it reaches the top and then take it sideways. At the same time, remove all other side shoots except those that lie next to a wire or batten. Gradually allow these side shoots to grow sideways until they meet those of the next tree. See the illustrations on the right for a more detailed analysis of the pruning cuts.

Established pruning

Once the pleached trees are established and the hedge or tunnel is completed, then the supports can be removed. Subsequent pruning is as for any other hedge. Aim to keep the growth tight and well clipped. Remove any new shoots pointing in the wrong direction that may appear on the trunks.

ABOVE A walkway of young trees that have been allowed to grow together instead of being pleached, but which give the same effect.

TRAINING PLEACHED TREES

The essence of pleaching is to create what is, in effect, an aerial hedge. The branches of the trees are encouraged to grow until they become intermingled, but they are grown entirely in one plane. This creates an eye-catching garden feature.

YEAR ONE Train the young trees against firmly planted posts with taut wires between them. Remove the bottom side shoots and tie the remainder into the wires, one to each wire.

YEAR TWO Continue to tie the new shoots to the wires as they appear. Tie in the existing side branches as they grow. Remove any other side shoots.

YEAR THREE OR LATER Interweave the side branches as they meet. Remove any extra side shoots from the main trunk and any from the main branches that go in the wrong direction or cause crowding.

Ornamental Shrubs

Shrubs are the backbone of a garden. They provide structure and form, as well as continuity throughout the seasons. Most flower at some point during the year but they are often grown just for their foliage, which may be decorative, act as a background to other plants, or provide a screen to what lies beyond.

Many gardeners simply turn a blind eye to pruning and let the shrubs get on with it. This policy often works for a limited number of years, but after a while the shrubs begin to outgrow their allotted space, as well as becoming leggy and full of dead wood. Unpruned, shrubs often lose their flower power and the number of blooms diminishes over the years. Regular pruning is not an arduous task and it certainly produces healthier and more productive as well as better-shaped shrubs.

Gardeners often tremble at the thought of pruning shrubs, but it is not at all complicated and the necessary skills are quickly learnt. Besides, you only have to know how to prune your own plants, not all the thousands of different ones that are in cultivation, so it soon becomes such a routine operation as cutting a hedge or mowing a lawn.

LEFT Ornamental shrubs form the backbone of any garden design, but should be pruned to control their shape and size to ensure that they continue to fit harmoniously together.

Initial training

Many shrubs that you buy from garden centres and nurseries are already trained to a basic shape, and these usually need little more than to be planted. But sometimes they need a bit of attention, especially those that have been lifted as seedlings or layers from your own or a friend's garden.

Buying shrubs

The same principles that apply to buying trees also apply to shrubs. In the first place, always buy healthy plants that are neither diseased nor harbouring pests. Never buy a sickly plant or one whose roots are wound into a tight ball. Try to choose a plant with well-balanced growth, avoiding anything that is drawn or too leggy. Do not automatically

ABOVE *Indigofera* is an attractive flowering shrub but one that benefits from good pruning. Left unpruned, its beauty diminishes.

select the largest plant on display as large plants in containers will not necessarily grow away quickly and fill their allotted space. Medium or even smaller ones will grow away faster and can soon overtake a larger one as they have a more balanced root to top-growth ratio.

Container and bare-root plants

Most shrubs are purchased in containers and can be planted at any time of year, as long as they are not allowed to dry out or scorch in hot sun before they have time to establish. However, a number of specialist nurseries, especially those dealing with roses and those who supply mail-order plants, provide them "bare-root". Bare-root plants are dug from nursery beds and sent to the customer, as the name suggests, with bare roots, i.e. not potted up in compost (soil mix). These are usually grown in rows in the nursery and are not necessarily given much in the way of initial pruning. They may need a bit more attention once they are planted. The advantage of bare-root shrubs is that

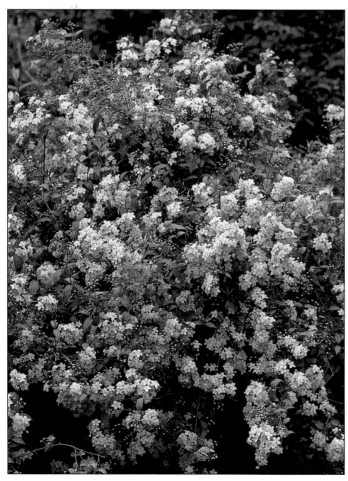

ABOVE Initial pruning helps to shape the shrub so that it makes the maximum impact. This *Deutzia elegantissima* would always be welcome.

ABOVE This *Viburnum opulus* is at the height of its powers and is a mass of flowers. Initial training helps to increase its flowering capacity.

they are usually cheaper, as they have not been handled or processed as much as containerized ones. Bare-root plants are usually only sold from mid-autumn to mid-spring, which is the best time for planting them.

Initial pruning and training

The aim of shaping any shrub, apart from topiary, is to let it achieve its natural habit. When shrubs are received from the nursery, most will already be trained in this fashion. Some may be badly formed, however, and need some remedial treatment as soon as they are planted. Remove any weak growth and if necessary cut out any crossing branches. If the shrub is to be dense and rounded in shape, cut back the shoots to a strong bud or pair of buds so that they branch out. As the shrub begins to grow it is likely to produce new growth from the base. Make certain that this is evenly spaced and cut out any crossing branches. Other than this, if a good specimen has been purchased in the first place, there should be no need for further pruning.

PLANTING AND PRUNING A YOUNG SHRUB

1 Prepare the soil well around the whole planting area so that the roots settle down quickly and produce a healthy plant.

2 Most shrubs are planted at the same depth as they were originally grown, either in their nursery bed or in the container in which they were purchased.

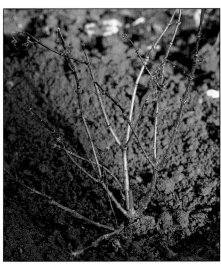

3 Some shrubs are already pruned, so they need no attention at all. Other shrubs have broken branches, weak growth and other defects that need correcting.

4 Remove any flowered wood back to a strong bud or to a strong new shoot.

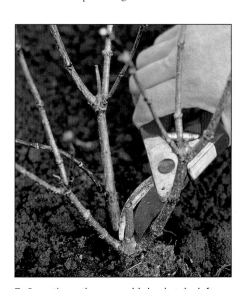

5 Sometimes there are old dead stubs left from previous pruning sessions, or wood that has become broken in transit. You will need to remove these.

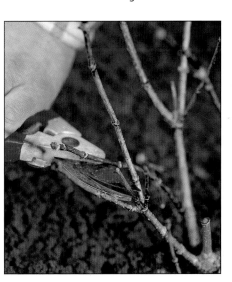

6 Often there will be inward-pointing shoots on the new shrub that are rubbing, or soon will rub, against other branches. You also need to cut these out.

7 The pruned plant should have a well-balanced, open basic framework from which the rest of the shrub will grow.

Established pruning

Once a shrub is fully established and growing away happily, it will need regular attention to keep it healthy and in shape. Many shrubs only need minimal treatment (a few can even be left to their own devices), but most need at least some attention.

Types of shrub

For pruning purposes, shrubs are usually divided into several categories: those that need no or minimal pruning (*Daphne, Ceanothus, Magnolia*), those that flower on the current year's growth (*Buddleja, Lavatera*), those that flower on the previous year's growth (*Forsythia, Philadelphus*) and those which are evergreen (*Elaeagnus, Osmanthus*). The main difference between the needs of the different categories is the timing of pruning and the amount required.

When to prune

Pruning is an ongoing activity, spread throughout the year, although the majority can be done in winter and spring. There is an old garden adage that says you should do things when you think of them, but although unlikely to kill the plant, pruning at the wrong time of year could at least curtail its flowering for the following season. For example, if you prune in the winter a shrub that flowers on the previous year's wood, you are likely to remove all the shoots that have flowering potential. These need time in the previous year to develop that wood and so should be pruned as soon after flowering as possible. Many of them, such as forsythia, are early flowering, leaving plenty of time for growth. The shrubs that flower on new wood are ones such as buddleja, which flower around mid- or late summer, once they have had a chance to produce new growth. These are usually best

ABOVE Not all shrubs need to be cut hard back. This *Ceanothus thyrsiflorus* only needs the longer new growth to be cut back by about a third after flowering.

pruned in the early spring. Evergreens usually only need minimal pruning, in spring.

Minimal pruning

In most cases, all that is needed is to look for and cut out any dead, dying or diseased wood. Some of these shrubs also benefit from being lightly trimmed over to reduce the length of the new growth, but only to prevent the shrub getting too large or outgrowing its position. If the shrub does get too large for its position, you can try cutting it back heavily. But often these shrubs will

Shrubs that need little or no pruning

Amelanchier	Daphne mezereum
Aronia arbutifolia	Enkianthus
Berberis	campanulatus
Callicarpa	Magnolia
bodinieri	Nandua (sacred
Calycanthus	bamboo)
Clerodendron	Phlomis
trichotomum	Rhododendron
Clethra alnifolia	(azalea)
Corylopsis	Salix helvetica
Crataegus	Salvia (sage)
(hawthorn)	Stephandra
Cytisus (broom)	Thymus (thyme)

Reversion

Sometimes shrubs with variegated leaves, most frequently evergreens, throw up a shoot which has reverted to the original green leaves of the parent species. If this shoot is ignored, it will gradually take over the whole bush and the variegation will be lost. So it is essential to cut out this green shoot at the base.

The reverse sometimes happens, where a green bush throws up a variegated shoot. If this is an interesting colour or pattern, it may be worthwhile taking a cutting and rooting it to see if you can produce a whole shrub with this variegation. This is how a lot of variegated plants are originally produced. Plain cream shoots that occasionally appear on variegated hollies are usually the result of cold weather. These cannot be used for propagation, as they lack chlorophyll.

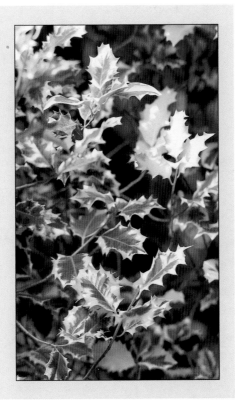

Shrubs flowering on old wood

Corylus (hazel)	(beauty bush)
Cotinus (smoke bush)	Philadelphus (mock orange)
Forsythia	Ribes
Hydrangea	sanguineum
Kerria (Jew's mantle)	(flowering currant)
Kolkwitzia	Rubus (bramble)

Shrubs flowering on old and new wood

These two categories of shrub are basically treated in the same way, the only major difference being the timing. Firstly, remove any dead, damaged or diseased wood. Take out any branches that cross over others. These may be rubbing against each other or just producing congestion, preventing the circulation of air and light. Any thin weak growths that are not going to produce healthy shoots should also be taken out. You can

not make new growth from old wood, so you may have to remove it altogether and start again. Occasionally you may need to cut out an individual shoot that has suddenly decided to grow faster than the others and spoils the shape of the shrub.

PRUNING SHRUBS THAT FLOWER ON THE PREVIOUS SEASON'S GROWTH

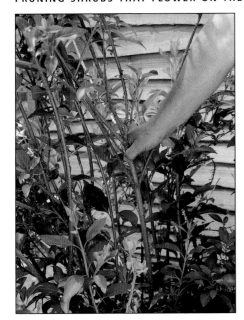

1 The best time to prune is soon after flowering. Count the number of stems and decide which third look the oldest (these will usually be the thickest and darkest).

2 Cut back the oldest third just above ground if the branches rise from ground level or to a stump near the base if there is thick old wood. Cut just above a new shoot near the plant base.

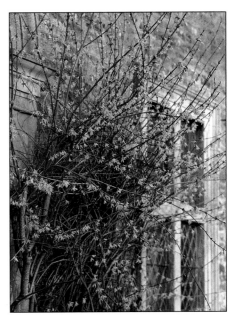

ABOVE If this forsythia is pruned after it has flowered in the spring, then plenty of replacement shoots will grow during the summer to flower the following year.

PRUNING SHRUBS THAT FLOWER ON THE CURRENT SEASON'S GROWTH

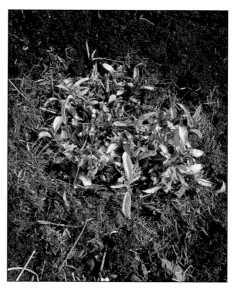

1 Many shrubs, such as this hardy fuchsia, flower on the current season's growth. In spring, all the older material that flowered the previous year will have to be cut out.

2 During the spring this old growth is cut back – as far as the ground in the case of the fuchsia. In other shrubs it may just be back to the first sound bud or shoot.

3 Once growth starts again, new shoots appear and quickly grow to flowering size. These require no further pruning until the following spring.

promote new healthy growth by removing some of the older wood. Old shoots, which are usually easy to identify, should be removed to the base, but if they are already producing vigorous new growth from just above the base, cut just above these new shoots. Take out a few of these older stems so that the bush retains its shape and appearance. If necessary, you can remove up to a third of the bush annually, so that over a three-year period a new shrub is formed. Normally it is only necessary to do this every few years, when the shrub has become congested or tired. Finally, look at the shrub to assess its shape and see if any of the remaining shoots need trimming to improve its overall appearance. It may be that some of the longer stems need cutting back to contain its size.

Evergreens

Most evergreens need very little pruning other than the routine removal of any dead, dying and diseased wood. They may need to be lightly trimmed over each year in order to maintain the size if that is important in the context of your garden. If the foliage is variegated, as in the case of some hollies, it is also important to remove any shoots that revert to the original green.

Shrubs flowering on new wood

Buddleja	Hypericum
Caryopteris	calycinum
Cassia	Indigofera
Ceanothus 'Gloire	Lavatera
de Versailles'	Leycesteria
Ceratostigma	Potentilla
Fuchsia	Sambucus (elder)

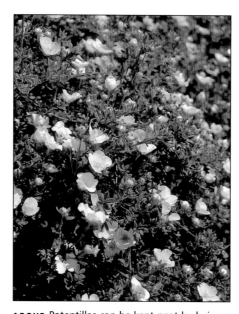

ABOVE Potentillas can be kept neat by being trimmed over after flowering. Apart from taking out the odd old stem to keep the plant vigorous, little other pruning is required.

Evergreen shrubs

Abelia	Garrya
Azara	Hebe
Berberis	Laurus nobilis
Buxus (box)	(bay)
Camellia	Mahonia
Ceanothus	Osmanthus
Choisya ternata	Photinia
(Mexican	Pieris
orange	Pittosporum
blossom)	Prunus
Convolvulus	lusitanicus
cneorum	(Portuguese
Cotoneaster	laurel)
Daphne	Rhododendron
Elaeagnus	Sarcococca
Escallonia	Skimmia
Euonymus	(Christmas box)
fortunei	Viburnum tinus

PRUNING EVERGREEN SHRUBS

1 Evergreen shrubs usually need little pruning, but sometimes, as in the case of this bay (*Laurus nobilis*), they may need to have their shape checked or improved.

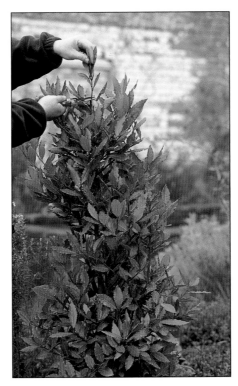

2 After you have removed any dead or damaged wood, look at the top of the shrub and cut back any straggly stems in order to improve its shape.

Deadheading

Most flowering shrubs benefit from deadheading. A plant requires a lot of energy in order to produce seed for reproduction. By removing the faded flowers, seeding is prevented and this energy is diverted into the new growth, sometimes producing a second flowering, which is always welcome. Another reason for deadheading your shrubs is that many of them look decidedly unsightly when they are covered with dead flowers, particularly those that have white flowers. As well as looking ugly themselves, dead flowers also tend to detract from the impact of those that are still at their best: remove the dead ones and then the look of the remainder will be greatly improved. Simply cut the flowering stem back to the first leaves as the flowers begin to fade.

3 Remove any long stems well back into the bush, as these could grow away and completely distort the shape of the plant.

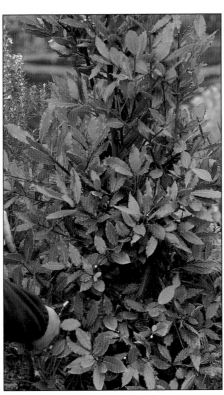

4 Then, complete the pruning by trimming back any wayward shoots near the base of the plant. The finished bush looks much tidier.

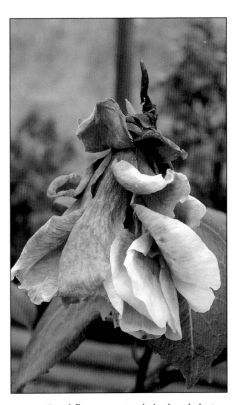

ABOVE Dead flowers not only look ugly but also detract from the remaining flowers. They will sap the plant's energy, so remove them.

Renovation pruning

It is not uncommon to be faced with a shrub that has not been pruned for many years, and is now in desperate need of renovation. Although the task may look daunting, it should not be a problem provided you take a systematic approach.

Clearing the way

The first stage, as with all pruning jobs, is to remove the dead wood. Next, take out any damaged, diseased or otherwise dying wood. In an overgrown shrub this often amounts to a great deal of material. Once it has been removed, the shrub already looks better and you can now see the framework you have to work on. Also remove any suckers around the plant. A neglected sumach (*Rhus*), for example, is likely to produce quite a number of suckers and these should be removed below ground level where the shoot joins the root.

If the shrub is badly diseased, it is best to remove it completely and start again, as it is highly unlikely that you will be able to resurrect it successfully.

RENOVATING AN OVERGROWN SHRUB Most shrubs can be renovated by removing dead wood and some of the oldest stems, as well as reducing the length of the remainder.

Reinvigoration

Remove any weak growth and any branches or stems that rub against or cross over other branches. The next thing to do is to try to reinvigorate the shrub. Remove some of the old wood to stimulate fresh new growth. Generally, several of the oldest main stems should be cut out completely or cut back to any new

REMOVING SUCKERS

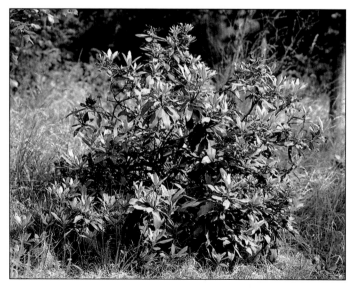

1 Some shrubs form a thicket as suckers grow around the base of the plant, often from the roots, but also from the base of the trunk.

2 Suckers should be removed by cutting them close to the trunk, or underground, close to the roots.

growth starting from near the base. Up to one-third of the oldest wood can be taken out. Repeat this process over the next three years until the shrub has completely regenerated itself. Some shrubs, such as *Ceanothus*, are reluctant to produce new growth from old wood. In this case, either omit this stage or remove the plant entirely and put a new one in its place.

Shaping up

A shrub that has been heavily pruned in this way is likely to be rather straggly and it may be necessary to reduce the remaining branches so that a better shape is achieved. The amount that can be removed will vary from shrub to shrub, but it can be up to about a half. However, some, such as *Ceanothus*, should only be trimmed over to remove the previous year's growth, as they will not reshoot from old wood.

Cutting down to the ground

There are some shrubs that can be simply cut to the ground and they will start again. Lilac (*Syringa*), elder

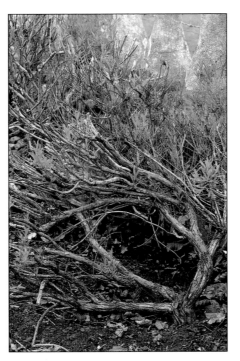

ABOVE Many shrubs that have grown straggly, such as this lavender, will not reshoot easily from old wood and should be replaced with new plants.

(*Sambucus*) and hazel (*Corylus*) are examples. Remove some of the top growth initially, so that the weight is removed from the main stems, then cut these off at about 15–30cm (6–12in) from the ground. If it is a grafted shrub, be certain to cut above the graft.

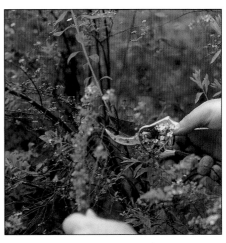

ABOVE With shrubs such as spiraea, you can remove one or two of the oldest shoots each year to promote the growth of new shoots.

Replacing

There are some shrubs that are virtually impossible to regenerate. If you cut back into the older wood, no new growth will appear and the plant will die. The best way to cope with this is to ensure that the shrubs are properly pruned in the first place and therefore do not become in need of renovation. However, if you inherit such overgrown plants when you move to a new garden, the only way to cope with them is to dig them out and replace them.

HOW TO RENOVATE A SHRUB

1 The first job when renovating any shrub is to cut out any dead branches or shoots right back to sound wood.

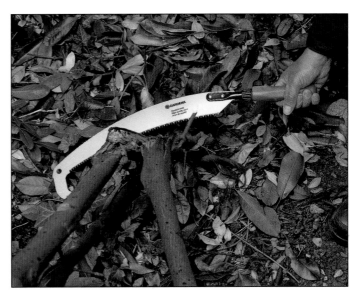

2 You need to remove any damaged wood, through which diseases can enter, as well as any dead wood.

Pruning for foliage effect

Some shrubs are grown mainly for their decorative foliage. It is possible to let these grow in the normal way and just give them a light pruning: they will still produce interesting foliage and will also produce flowers, often attractive ones, such as on the smoke bush (*Cotinus*). If, however, they are cut right back, the leaves will be larger and often of a more intense colour, giving the plant a more striking appearance.

What can be cut back?

Elder (*Sambucus*), *Rosa glauca* and the smoke bush (*Cotinus*) are all good examples of shrubs that benefit from a drastic pruning regime. *Eucalyptus gunnii* can become a very tall tree but if cut right back and treated as a shrub it produces very interesting juvenile foliage, which is much in demand by flower arrangers. Another interesting range of shrubs are those with decorative young stems. *Cornus stolonifera*, *C. alba* and the coloured-stemmed *Rubus* are good examples of these.

ABOVE A cotinus in full flower. If hard pruned in spring, the foliage will be larger and more colourful, but the flowers will be sacrificed.

Pruning for foliage

The most attractive foliage tends to appear on new growth, so all the old growth is removed, usually in late winter. This means that plenty of new shoots are produced in spring. All the plant's energy is thus put

Shrubs pruned for attractive foliage

Berberis	Philadelphus
Cotinus (smoke	coronarius
bush)	'Aureus'
Eucalyptus	Rosa glauca
gunnii	Sambucus (elder)

into the production of leaves and very little or none into flowers. Hence, the leaves are big and there are no flowers. Once the shrub is established it is surprising just how much growth is put on in one year. Although cut to the ground in spring, an elder (*Sambucus*) can grow 2.5–3m (8–10ft) in a season. This can be repeated for as many years as you like. If you decide that you want a larger shrub or want it to flower, just stop cutting it back each year.

It is normal to cut it to within about 30cm (12in) of the ground, but as the plant ages so the basal stems can be left longer. However, it is possible to treat it as a pollard

HOW TO PRUNE FOR FOLIAGE

1 Elder (*Sambucus*), like the cotinus above, can be pruned hard if you would like to have good foliage effect, or pruned lightly if you prefer the flowers.

2 Cut back all the previous year's growth to a strong bud within 30cm (12in) or so of the ground. This may seem drastic but the shrub will rapidly recover.

3 After many years of this treatment, the pruning will be too far from the ground and some stems should be cut back each year, almost to the ground.

to create a taller bush, perhaps at the back of a border where you want the foliage to be above the surrounding plants.

Pruning for stems

Decorative, coloured stems are at their best in the winter, when, of course, they can be most clearly seen and add interest to an otherwise barren garden. If the shrubs are left unpruned, they become large and the stem colour is confined to the short growths at the tips of the branches. However, if they are regularly cut to the ground each year, they will throw up a mass of thin shoots, each a strong colour – bright yellowish green, for example, in the case of *Cornus stolonifera* 'Flaviramea', and red in *C. alba* 'Sibirica'. The shoots are cut to the ground in spring, after which they quickly shoot and are fully grown by the following winter. These shrubs are unlikely to flower.

Some shrubs, such as the various brambles (*Rubus*), are grown entirely for their stems because the flowers are insignificant. The advantage of cutting these back in spring is not only to provide good stems the following winter, but also to make it much easier to weed and generally tidy up around them.

Shubs pruned for attractive winter bark

Cornus alba 'Sibirica'	Rubus thibetianus
Cornus stolonifera 'Flaviramea'	Salix alba subsp. vitellina 'Britzensis'
Rubus cockburnianus	Salix fargesii
	Salix irrorata

PRUNING FOR COLOURFUL STEMS

1 The winter stems of *Salix alba* subsp. *vitellina*. Left unpruned, the stems will get higher and the coloured part shorter.

2 Cut back some of the older wood to reduce congestion and rejuvenate the plant from the base. Use a saw on this thicker wood.

3 Remove any dead branches and shoots right back to sound wood. Use a saw for thicker wood and clean up the cuts.

4 By now you should be left with the basic framework of the shrub and have some idea as to how it will look next year.

5 Cut back any remaining last year's shoots to a good strong bud. This may seem drastic, but the shrub will soon recover.

6 If the shrub is at the front of a border or has another shrub behind it, aim to keep it lower, almost to the ground.

ABOVE Winter colour in cornus and salix stems. The tall shrubs in the background are losing their colour by becoming too large.

Topiary

There has been a very long tradition of shaping shrubs and trees into decorative forms that are at total variance with their natural shapes. The gardener imposes a very strict pattern on their growth, either by forcing the shrub into a shape by wiring it on to formers or by clipping existing branches to make and retain a shape. The shapes can vary from simple geometric ones, such as balls or pyramids, which work particularly well in formally designed gardens, to free-form designs, such as birds or animals, which can often be of a witty or whimsical nature. Living sculpture does a lot to enliven a garden, creating immediate interest and focal points that draw the eye. Topiary can be free-standing or incorporated into hedges and even archways. It can be used in containers, perhaps in matching pairs placed at strategic places such as near entrances or at the top or bottom of flights of steps.

Topiary is not difficult in itself, but the freer-form shapes may well need an artist's eye and hand to make them really effective. There are a few basic techniques, which are easy to learn, but perhaps the most difficult aspect is the patience that is required while waiting for the shrub to grow into shape.

Since topiary has to hold its shape for as long as possible without daily or weekly pruning, the shrubs employed have to have special qualities that make them suitable. Theoretically, almost any shrub could be used, but in reality there are only a handful that are really good for the job.

LEFT In the late Piet Bekaert's garden in Belgium, the artist's house sits at the centre of a visually arresting geometrical framework of topiary, clipped hedges and trees.

Pruning and training simple topiary

Topiary is not difficult but needs a steady hand and a keen eye. The tools are those that you would use for pruning or hedging, namely a pair of secateurs (pruners) and hedge clippers, preferably hand ones as these are easier to control.

Selecting shrubs

Evergreen shrubs that are slow-growing and have compact growth, such as yew (*Taxus*) or box (*Buxus*), are the best types to use. It is also an advantage to use shrubs that have small leaves, again such as box, as it is easier to obtain a smooth finish with these. However, shrubs with larger leaves such as holly (*Ilex*) or bay laurel (*Laurus nobilis*) are suitable for simple shapes such as balls. Shrubs for topiary can be already fully grown, and then "carved" into shape, but they are best grown especially for the purpose and gradually clipped into shape as they grow.

ABOVE Cones are among some of the easiest shapes to construct, even if they take a few years to grow. They always look effective and draw the eye.

Creating a simple shape

To create a simple shape such as a ball, cone or pyramid, start when the plant is relatively small and clip it into a smaller version of the shape you desire. Gradually increase the size as the plant grows. This approach will create many multi-branched shoots, which will become very dense and will not only hold the shape well, but will look better. If you wait for the plant to reach the intended size and then start cutting, it will take many years before it thickens out and becomes a solid shape, if it ever does. Once the plant reaches the size you want, cut it into its final shape, preferably using a former so that it is completely regular.

Spirals

These have sufficient presence to be used individually, but they also work well as matching pairs, perhaps flanking a front door or another entrance, and they can even be planted in small groups to great effect. Spirals differ in form quite dramatically, from full-bodied figures with voluptuous curves to those with slender coils which look like a leafy garland twisted around a bare pole.

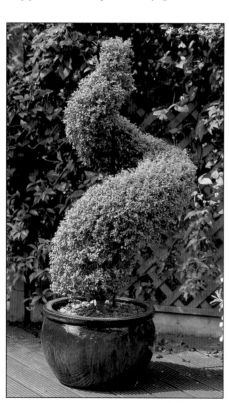

ABOVE A basic spiral made from box. Box is a good, compact shrub that holds its shape well and does not require a great deal of clipping.

ABOVE This relatively complicated shape is made possible by using a former, which will eventually become hidden.

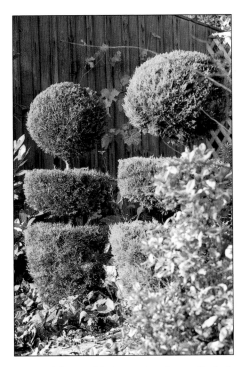

ABOVE It is possible to construct complicated geometric shapes that always catch the eye.

ABOVE These perfectly rounded box hummocks enhance both the shape of the pool and the serenity of the formal garden in which they are situated.

The slender-coiled kind can be tricky because they demand more skill from the topiarist and take longer to train than the full-bodied kind, which can be clipped almost instantly. You will often see them grown from relatively quick-growing conifers such as juniper, thuja and chamaecyparis. They also tend to be quite expensive to buy. However, some of these swirling forms are not as difficult to create as you might think. Box is ideal for clipping small to medium-size spirals in containers, but yew is better for producing large specimens grown in the ground.

When training a spiral, you can put your own stamp on to the design because there are several variables. At one extreme there is the squat snail shell, which has broad coils and only a shallow-cut groove. This means that the coils lie on top of each other with no gaps. Imagine attaching a string to the tip and pulling upwards to separate the coils slightly: you then have the next variant, whereby the coils are set at a more pronounced angle. This angle, coupled with the width of the coils, suggests varying degrees of motion, from lazy turns to dynamic twists. Sometimes a spiral groove is clipped into a column instead of a cone, and you can also create near-horizontal coils clipped to resemble a gentle helter-skelter.

Whatever shape you decide on, do not worry if your spiral is not

ABOVE Topiary can also be great fun. Your imagination is the only limit when it comes to ideas. Avoid too many wacky shapes in one garden, however, as it can become boring.

mathematically perfect or if an existing topiary begins to drift from the original design, with a pronounced lean or unravelling top. Topiary often ends up being quirky or eccentric.

Standard trees and shrubs

There are two types of standard. One consists of usually prostrate or low-growing shrubs that are grafted on to the trunk of an upright-growing shrub. This type is generally purchased already trained. The other type involves training just one central stem by removing other competing stems and then pinching out any side shoots, just leaving those on the top to develop into a rounded bush. Good subjects for this treatment are the firethorn (*Pyracantha*) and the bay laurel (*Laurus nobilis*). Once fully grown, both types need regular trimming to keep their shape. In

general, such standards are grown simply as balls, for example the popular bay laurels often seen flanking doorways or paths, but they can also be cut into more complex shapes.

With a shape such as a simple globe, dome, cone or stylized bird held at the top of a slender stem, the topiary standard is certainly elegant. Whatever the design, topiary standards will add a touch of style to your garden. Consider them as potted sculptures for the terrace, rising up above a sea of planting in the border or paired with an identical twin to frame a gateway. Many gardeners have experience of making standards using quick-growing tender perennials such as fuchsias and marguerite daisies (*Argyranthemum*), and the same techniques are used for creating standards of box, bay, holly and so on.

Suitable shrubs

Bay (*Laurus nobilis*)
Box (*Buxus sempervirens*)
Firethorn (*Pyracantha*)
Holly (*Ilex*)
Ivy (*Hedera*)
Privet (*Ligustrum ovalifolium*)
Shrubby honeysuckle (*Lonicera nitida*)
Yew (*Taxus baccata*)

Maintenance

Cut the topiary as required to keep the shape with a smooth outline. Use a former for precise geometric shapes to ensure that the outline is kept regular. Formers can be constructed from lengths of wood or from a sheet of wood cut to shape. Freer shapes such as spirals can be cut by winding a length of string down the shrub, then cutting to this. Trim complicated shapes by following the shape of the former within the plant.

TRAINING A TOPIARY CONE

1 Choose a relatively small, young plant which has evenly spaced branches. It should have a clear upright stem at the centre. Push a cane into the pot to guide the training.

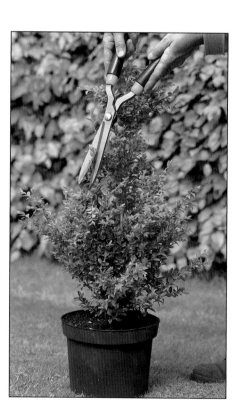

2 Use hand shears to shape the branches. Work from the top, keeping a smooth and regular outline that widens out at the bottom of the plant.

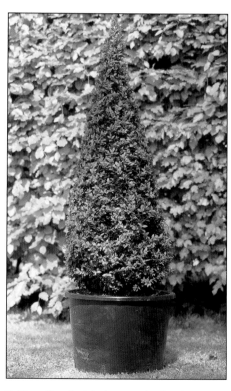

3 Allow the plant to increase in size, but continue clipping the branches to keep the cone shape. This will create many multi-branched shoots that will hold the shape well.

CLIPPING A DOUBLE BALL

1 Buy a mature, dense, bushy plant with a clear upright stem at the centre. It must be the correct height for the final tree as it will fill out rather than grow taller.

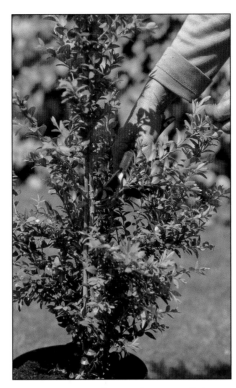

2 Using secateurs (pruners) remove all the branches from the centre of the stem, making clean cuts. Leave enough shoots at the top and bottom to shape the double balls.

3 Start shaping the bottom ball by shortening the side shoots to form a rough ball. Cut out the shoot tip of the leading growth to encourage side shoots to form.

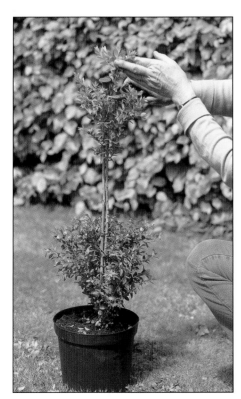

4 Shape the top ball in the same way, cutting the main shoot tip and pinching out the other shoot tip buds. Make sure the top remains securely attached to the supporting cane.

5 Use shears to clip to the final shape. Flip the shears over so that the blades follow the curve of the ball. Continue to pinch off any leaves or shoots that appear on the stem.

6 Until it is well-established, it is advisable to place the tree in a sheltered spot away from direct sunlight and wind. This mature specimen looks striking against a beech hedge.

Pruning and training more complex shapes

While simple shapes, such as spheres and obelisks, can be very pleasing, particularly in formal situations, more complex shapes, such as animals or birds, add a touch of excitement, and even danger, to the art. Perhaps it is not something for the faint-hearted but until you try it you won't really know whether you can do it or not. A little artistic flair and imagination help, but many examples have been created by gardeners who would certainly never consider themselves as artists or sculptors.

Deciding what to do
The first difficulty is choosing a subject. The best place to look for inspiration is at existing topiary. Some gardens are famous for it and they are well worth a visit. Take a notebook and make sketches from different angles. If possible, take a look inside and see if there is any supporting structure. Another source, albeit only two-dimensional, is pictures in books and magazines, both of topiary and of everyday objects that could be subjects for topiary. Finally, you could pay a visit to the local garden centre and see what pre-shaped formers they have.

ABOVE This miniature knot garden is an unusual design. It need not be as complicated as it looks. Imagination and a steady hand are basically all that is needed.

Shrubs
With most forms of topiary, slow- and compact-growing shrubs are the best to choose. These hold their shapes better and tend to grow at an even pace all over the shape. Avoid large-leaved shrubs as these are difficult to cut into complex shapes.

Making complex shapes
The first task after planting your shrub is to build a former and erect it over the shrub. This can simply be a number of sticks or rods wired together, one for each main limb of the topiary. Attach branches to these as they grow, and then gradually trim them as they fill out so that the overall shape is formed. Another method is to make the complete shape out of chicken wire and then prune back the emerging branches about 2.5cm (1in) or so outside it. Keep pruning regularly at this distance so that the shrub bushes out and thickens, eventually filling out the shape completely. Although it is not to be generally

CLIPPING A PIG FREEHAND

1 Ingenuity and creativity are two of the key elements in producing interesting pieces of topiary. Seeing a pig in this box shrub is a stroke of genius.

2 You must have a clear idea of what you are doing before you start clipping. You should work out where all the main elements are going to go.

3 The finished pig makes an eye-catching feature in this winter garden. Unlike a marble sculpture, if you do make a mistake while clipping, you can wait until it grows again.

CLIPPING A TOPIARY BIRD IN A NEST

1 Choose a squat, bushy plant with plenty of dense foliage. Select suitable stems for the head and tail of the bird and tie these together with raffia or string.

2 Set the tail at the desired angle, using string and a tent peg in the ground. Using shears, start shaping the bird by clipping out the foliage between the tail and head stems.

3 Trim the foliage at the sides to create the curve of the bird's body. Shake out the bush as you work to release clippings that may be caught behind others.

4 Using secateurs (pruners), you can then go on to shape the head and neck of the bird. To train the beak, simply twist a small length of garden wire around the soft wood.

5 Again using shears, cut away branches at the bottom of the plant to form the nest. Remember to feed and water the topiary regularly to encourage recovery.

6 The finished bird in a nest looks effective in a terracotta pot placed in a simple setting – here, in front of a beech hedge. The tail is beautifully silhouetted against the backdrop.

recommended, some people start with an existing, full-grown shrub and just sculpt away. At first this can look a bit bare and sparse in places but new leaves and shoots will soon grow and it will thicken out to the shape required.

Maintaining complex shapes

Once you have achieved the shape you require it is essential that you keep pruning it to that shape. If you leave it too long, shoots will lengthen, often at different rates. If you simply shear off 15cm (6in) all over, you will end up with a

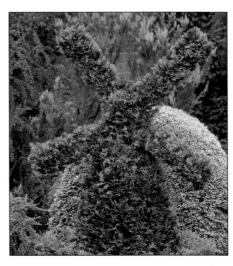

ABOVE After spending so much time creating your topiary specimen, you will want to ensure it is well kept and maintained.

distorted shape. Leave the former inside and, using this as a guide, try to cut back to a regular distance over the whole topiary.

If, for some reason, you miss a year's trimming you may have a monumental task to get it back into shape. It pays to take photographs from different angles so that you have an accurate idea of what it was like. Alternatively, a drawing with measurements will help you find your way back to the original. Often, you can just make out the line of the older wood which indicates the original shape.

Quick topiary

In general, most topiary is created from slow-growing shrubs such as yew or box as these are dense and retain their shape well. However, the downside of using such plants is that it may take several years for them to reach their ultimate shape and possibly more for them to thicken up to make a solid sculpture. One way of speeding up the process is to use a fast-growing climber instead, such as ivy (*Hedera*).

Ivy for speed

One of the reasons topiaried ivy is so quick to create is that it only covers the outside of the framework and does not have to form a dense mass – a bit like making a hollow papier-mâché head as opposed to carving one in solid wood or marble. Although ivy is fast growing, it is also good at holding its shape and therefore does not need too much attention once the shape is formed.

Formers

This form of topiary has become popular, and garden centres and nurseries have responded by offering a good range of differently shaped formers over which to grow the ivy. The better-quality ones are made from thick wire or even steel, while cheaper ones are available made from chicken wire. There is a vast range of designs, varying from geometric shapes to animals. Most have strong

TRAINING AN IVY BALL

1 Place one wire hanging basket on a flower pot for balance. Line the inside with moistened moss and fill with compost (soil mix).

2 Repeat the process with a second basket. Place the two basket frames firmly together and tie with wire twists.

3 Using a sharpened peg or cane, poke holes in the moss and plant ivy cuttings in a circular direction, starting from the top.

4 Once you have planted most of the cuttings, hang the basket and finish the underside of the topiary ball, filling in any gaps.

TRAINING AN IVY CONE

1 Plant seven small ivy plants with long trails (here, *Hedera helix* 'Ardingly') around the edge of the pot at even intervals.

2 Take your chosen topiary frame and gently place it in the pot, securing it carefully with your hands in the soil.

3 Carefully tease out each trail of ivy, and wind them up the sides and around the struts of the frame. Secure them with ties.

4 Pinch out the growing tips and tuck in the ends; this will encourage side shoots and bushiness. Trim when needed.

TRAINING AN IVY HEART

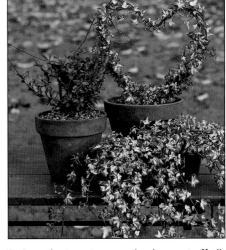

1 You can make 2-D frames from pieces of stout wire. Plant ivies on each side of the pot and then push the frame into the potting mix. Start to weave the ivies around the frame.

2 Continue to weave the trailing ivy stems up and around the wire frame, tucking in the strands as you go. Tie in with small pieces of string if this is necessary.

3 Once the two stems are in place, cut off all other trailing parts of the plant. The foliage will gradually thicken out to cover the wire frame completely.

legs or feet which are pushed into the ground, but some are much taller and include shapes on top of tripods or obelisks, the entire structure being covered with ivy. There is no reason why you should not create your own. Simple shapes are easy to make out of chicken wire and if you are good with your hands there is no reason why you should not attempt to create more complex shapes such as birds or animals. There is also no need to restrict yourself to static animals. A fox can be running or a bird can be in flight. You can be witty and combine several animals in a group on a lawn, for example.

Choosing ivy

Normally only one ivy plant is required, though to create larger shapes it will be quicker if two or more are used. You can use any type of ivy, either green or variegated, although the smaller-leaved varieties are best as the overall shape is smoother. There is no reason why two different ivies, say a green and a gold form, cannot be used to create

an even more effective sculpture, a sheep with a green body and yellow head for example.

Planting and shaping

Plant the ivy and then place the framework over it. As the stems grow, tie them in so that they eventually cover the whole shape. Once an area is covered, trim off any stray shoots and continue until the whole frame is covered. Regularly trim off any shoots that stick out, so that a recognizable shape is maintained.

Suggestions for formers and shapes

balls	ducks	teapots
cubes	herons	windmills
pyramids	dogs	boats
cones	sheep	aeroplanes
obelisks	cows	cars
moons	camels	pigs
birds	foxes	peacocks
swans	ponies	stars
geese	cats	horses

Hedges

Hedges are a good alternative to walls and fences as a method of sealing off your boundaries or creating individual areas or screening within a garden. A hedge is relatively cheap, but like all plants in a garden it is a living thing and will need a certain amount of time spent on it to keep it in shape.

As well as their use as physical barriers, hedges also make visual ones, creating backdrops against which to grow other plants. Internal hedges can also be used to create an air of mystery, as a visitor is never quite certain what lies just beyond and always has the urge to move further into the garden, just to see what is there.

Unlike walls and fences, of course, hedges grow and so need trimming from time to time. Generally, this is a relatively easy procedure and there is a wide variety of equipment available to help you carry it out. Some hedging plants are slow-growing and it can take several years to achieve a mature hedge. However, they only need one or possibly two trims a year. Fast-growing shrubs, on the other hand, produce a hedge quickly but need more frequent pruning to look neat.

LEFT Neat hedges and archways can make a garden, providing not only screens but also a background for other plantings. Their formal shape makes an effective foil to the display of flowers in the borders.

Creating a hedge

Many hedges are inherited, but you may be lucky enough to have the chance to create a hedge from scratch. There is a range of texture and colour as well as styles of hedge that might influence your decision.

Types of hedge

There are two basic types of hedge (with a few minor variations). The majority of hedges can be called formal. They are composed of tight-growing shrubs that are kept neatly clipped. Informal hedges are allowed to grow in their natural way, usually with long stems arching over. These look very casual and have the advantage that their flowering stems are not removed. Not only will they flower at some point during the year, but they may also provide colourful fruit. They are usually pruned only once a year, or even once every two years. They do take up more space, however, so are best restricted to internal hedges, otherwise relations with neighbours might become somewhat strained.

Sub-categories are really only variations of these. Country hedges often contain a number of different types of shrub. The variation of textures and colours looks attractive

ABOVE Hedging plants come in several ages. Biggest is not always best as the smaller ones often establish more quickly and catch up.

but the growth rate of the different types varies, so the hedge can look rather ragged unless it is clipped frequently. Another type is the tapestry hedge, which is composed of different varieties of the same type

Informal hedging plants

Berberis	Rosa (rose)
Escallonia*	Tamarix
Forsythia	(tamarisk)
Fuchsia	Viburnum*
Garrya*	
Ribes sanguineum	
(flowering currant)	* Evergreen

ABOVE When buying, it is much cheaper to obtain hedging material bare-rooted, direct from the ground, rather than in containers.

of shrub. This provides a patchwork of colour when, for example, green and golden yews are used.

Consider whether you want an evergreen hedge or a deciduous one that is transparent in winter. Finally, hedges can be categorized by use. Hawthorn (*Crataegus*), holly (*Ilex*) and berberis all provide thick prickly hedges that are good for keeping livestock and other intruders out. Yew, on the other hand, produces a hedge that provides a superb backdrop for other plants.

Planting a hedge

Hedges are usually grown from bare-root plants bought from specialist nurseries, as the quantity required makes container-grown shrubs prohibitively expensive. They are usually available for planting from late autumn to early spring.

DIFFERENT TYPES OF HEDGE

ABOVE Yew makes a tight hedge that is particularly suitable for neat formal hedging. It only needs cutting once a year.

ABOVE Garrya makes an attractive informal hedge, with its dangling cream tassels. Too much pruning would spoil the shape.

ABOVE Most conifer hedges need to be clipped regularly to stop them becoming too large, when they will be difficult to renovate.

HOW TO CREATE A NEW HEDGE

The more thorough the preparation before planting and pruning the hedge, the better the hedge will eventually be. First of all, dig the ground well and add plenty of well-rotted organic material. Hawthorn, also known as quickthorn, is, as its name implies, one of the quickest as well as one of the most impenetrable plants with which to create a hedge.

YEAR ONE Hawthorn plants should be cut back soon after planting to encourage them to branch at the base and produce a thicker hedge.

YEAR TWO Cut back the resulting shoots so that these also branch. Keep repeating this until a thick hedge has been formed.

For a narrow hedge, set plants at 30cm (12in) intervals (use a wider spacing for more vigorous shrubs). For a wider and more substantial hedge they can be planted in two staggered rows, about 30cm (12in) apart, at 45cm (18in) intervals. The ground should be well prepared in advance. Remove any perennial weeds and dig in plenty of organic material. When planting a hedge, leave a gap between the hedge and any border that is to lie in front of it. This will allow you access to the hedge for cutting.

ABOVE A holly hedge takes a long time to get going, but eventually forms a good-looking, impenetrable screen or barrier.

Initial pruning and training

Advice for this tends to vary with fashion, but most deciduous hedging, such as beech and hornbeam, should only be lightly cut back on planting, no more than a third. Faster-growing shrubs, such as hawthorn and privet (*Ligustrum*), should be cut back low down, to 30cm (12in) or even less above the ground to make them bush out. Evergreens generally only need to have any overlong shoots cut back, leaving the leaders to achieve their finished height before they are stopped. As the hedge nears its final shape, keep trimming back any shoots that extend beyond the desired profile.

Formal hedging plants

Beech (*Fagus*)	Holly (*Ilex*)*
*Elaeagnus**	Privet
*Euonymus**	(*Ligustrum*)*
Hemlock (*Tsuga*)*	Portuguese laurel
Hornbeam	(*Prunus*
(*Carpinus*)	*lusitanica*)*
	Yew (*Taxus*)*
*Evergreen	

ABOVE An interesting pattern can be created by using shrubs with differing foliage colours. They are known as tapestry hedges.

ABOVE Mixed hedges produce an interesting texture but the shrubs often grow at different rates and need frequent pruning.

ABOVE Informal hedges, such as pyracantha, need less clipping and have the added advantage of flowers, but can look untidy.

Maintaining hedges

Hedges have to be cut regularly in order not only to keep them neat and tidy to look at, but also to prevent wayward stems whipping against people as they walk past.

Tools

There is now an extraordinary range of tools for cutting hedges. Hand shears are still the favourite of many gardeners who only have small areas of hedging to cut, as well as of those who like a more controlled method of trimming. Mechanical hedge trimmers, powered by either electricity or petrol engines, are widely available and relatively cheap. It is much quicker to cut a hedge using these, but, equally, any mistake is usually much more noticeable than one made with hand shears. Electric trimmers are lighter and cheaper than petrol ones, but you are restricted by the length of cable (unless you have a small, movable generator to produce the power). Cordless machines are available, but their power supply, and hence cutting time, is limited. Petrol ones are much

ABOVE This formal yew hedge has been immaculately maintained. Achieving a hedge as straight and neat as this needs a good eye as well as regular practice.

heavier, but these are more versatile in that they can be used anywhere without a power lead. They are also more powerful, cutting through most, even overgrown, hedging material. Gardeners with a lot of hedging would do well to invest in professional-standard machines, which cost a little more but are much better machines. New on the market are petrol cutters on extended poles. These can be very heavy to use, but allow the gardener to reach high hedges without the need for ladders

or scaffolds. Since it is possible to alter the angle of the head, they can also be used to reach hedges over ditches or narrow flower beds.

Another technical development that is especially useful to gardeners with tall hedges to maintain is the availability of scaffolds and specially designed stepladders that enable safe access to the tops of high hedges. These are expensive and sometimes cumbersome, but are easier and far safer to use than conventional ladders.

PRUNING FORMAL HEDGES

Formal hedges, whether they are flat-topped or have curved tops, need regular clipping in order to keep them compact and under control. If they are at the front of the house, you will also want to keep them looking neat and tidy. Remember always to try to clip back to the previous contour of the hedge or it will gradually get larger.

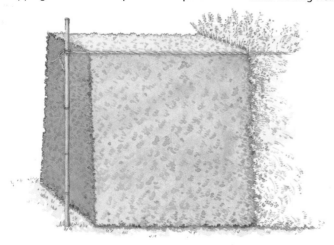

FLAT-TOPPED FORMAL HEDGES A flat-sided and flat-topped hedge has very distinct, clear-cut lines. The base should be a little wider than the top.

FORMAL HEDGES WITH CURVED TOPS An alternative to the flat top is to use a curved one, which is less formal. One advantage of this shape is that it is better at shedding snow.

PRUNING A FORMAL HEDGE

1 Quick-growing formal hedges will need trimming several times a year, but many evergreen hedges remain respectable with just one or two cuts during the year.

2 The clippings are easier to deal with if you lay a plastic sheet along the base of the hedge. You will be able to pick up most of them easily by gathering up the sheet.

3 If you are using hand shears, try to keep the blades flat against the side of the hedge. If you cut with a stabbing motion, then the finish is likely to be uneven.

4 Achieving a level top can be difficult. String stretched taut between two canes can make all the difference. Remember to have the guide low enough to allow for growth.

5 Try to hold the blades of the shears flat and horizontal when you are cutting the top. This may mean standing on steps or even a raised plank resting on two sets of steps.

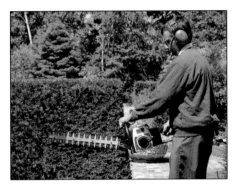

6 Power tools can make the job easier, but you should use goggles, gloves and ear protectors. Use the hedge trimmer with a wide, sweeping motion, keeping the blade parallel to the hedge.

Templates

A final piece of useful equipment is a template, something you will have to make yourself, as every hedge is unique in terms of size and shape. If you have a good eye or are not too bothered about precision, then it is possible to cut a hedge without a guide, but if you are not careful the hedge can get bigger and bigger as you cut just outside the previous line each time. A simple folding guide can be made from lengths of batten, joined with string. Use long pieces to mark the sides of the hedge. Attach a shorter piece to the end of each to mark the top of the hedge. Stretch strings between points on each of the guides to allow you to cut to the same profile each time. If you only cut one side of the

7 Some conifers produce stray vigorous side shoots, and simply nipping these off with secateurs (pruners) may be enough to improve the appearance between proper trims.

8 This carefully clipped yew hedge displays all the graceful formality and strength of a well-maintained hedge.

hedge, two uprights with strings attached will suffice. Alternatively, make one guide and move it along the hedge as you cut. For low box hedges or to shape a hedge top, cut the templates from sheets of plywood.

You can cut a hedge to whatever shape you like, but it is usual to have straight sides that narrow towards the top to allow maximum light to reach the leaves at the bottom. However, there is no reason why the top should not be wavy or irregular.

ABOVE Beech hedges only need cutting once or twice a year and have the advantage of holding on to their dead leaves all winter.

Formal hedges

These are usually cut tight to produce a dense, solid face. Depending on the type of hedging material, they will require from one to four cuts a year. For an even more sheer appearance, they can be cut more often. In general, they are best cut with hand shears or power tools. Regular trimming is easier if the hedge is no higher than can be comfortably cut from the ground. This saves a lot of time and effort and is, of course, much safer as no ladders or scaffolds are needed. However, if taller hedges are required as screens, windbreaks or simply as backdrops, then some means of elevation will be necessary. Use a template to ensure that the hedge is cut to a regular shape.

Semi-formal hedges

There are some hedges that, although regularly trimmed to a tight shape, are a little more ragged. This is because they are composed of plants that have larger leaves, such as laurel (*Prunus*), which cannot present the tight, cropped appearance of yew or box. These are cut in the same way as formal hedges, although you should really cut them with a pair of secateurs (pruners). Shears or trimmers will cut many of the leaves in half, which looks ugly and leads to a brown line along the cut edge.

ABOVE Tightly cut formal hedges always contrast well with informal backgrounds and are perfect as a backdrop to borders.

PRUNING AN INFORMAL FLOWERING HEDGE These hedges need little clipping other than to take off the flowered stems and any overlong shoots. A loose shape is what to aim for.

PRUNING AN INFORMAL HEDGE

1 Most flowering hedges are best trimmed when the flowers have finished. Exceptions are where attractive fruits or berries will follow, such as *Rosa rugosa*.

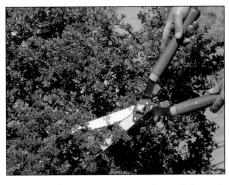

2 The simplest way to prune a large, informal hedge is with hand shears or a powered hedge trimmer. Only do this with small-leaved plants, such as berberis, though.

3 Although taking longer, secateurs will do a better job, especially with large-leaved plants. To restrict size, cut back overlong shoots to a suitable replacement shoot or cut out entirely.

Informal hedges

These are not trimmed or cut in the normal manner. Instead, the stems are allowed to arch gently as they would on a single shrub. Some pruning is required or they will soon become overgrown. In order to ensure flowering, they are treated in exactly the same way as single shrubs: those that flower on new wood are cut back in spring and those that flower on the previous year's wood are pruned after flowering.

4 (*above*) Shortening long shoots each year will keep most informal hedges looking good.

5 (*right*) The shrub roses usually used for hedges do not require heavy pruning. If they become congested, cut out the oldest and thickest stems close to the base.

General maintenance

It is important for the health and shape of a hedge that weeds, especially woody ones such as brambles, are not allowed to grow up through it. You should regularly strim underneath the hedge, cutting off weeds and grass, and dig out any brambles or alien shrubs or trees that have seeded themselves. Ivy seed can be dispersed by birds and then the ivy climbs through and over the hedge, possibly even killing it. It may then collapse itself, leaving a large hole. Remove it as soon as you see it, even if you think it looks rather attractive.

Heavy falls of snow should be knocked from hedgetops, as the weight can pull the stems out of shape.

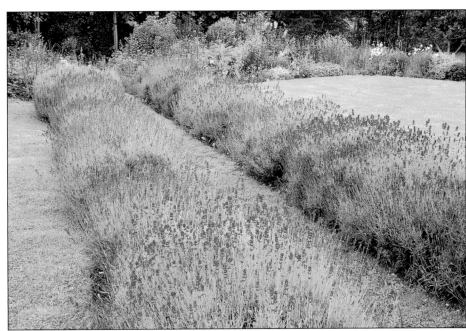

ABOVE Two lavender hedges bordering a path give the garden a wonderfully informal quality and provide a useful feature in cottage gardens.

Shaped hedges and arches

The conventional hedge has straight sides and a level top. The crispness and evenness appeals to many gardeners and a well-cut hedge is often taken as a sign of a skilled gardener. There is, however, no holy writ that says that hedges should be so geometrically shaped.

Uneven hedges

Without necessarily setting out to, some gardeners often end up with a hedge that is full of bulges and graceful curves, a bit like rolling surf. Initially, these may simply be hedges that have grown out of line, with some individual plants perhaps growing quicker than others, but as time passes the irregularities become more exaggerated and the rounded contour is a feature of the garden. Often, with age, the top becomes broader than the base and suddenly, perhaps because of snow or wind, branches are pushed apart and a split opens up in the hedge.

Shaped hedges

While an uneven hedge often just seems to occur spontaneously, it is possible to create a non-conventional hedge by design. A typical example would be one that has a crenellated or castellated top, like the battlements of a castle. To achieve this, allow alternate blocks of the hedge to grow taller. To create a wave effect, cut the top into a series of graceful mounds. The sides can also be shaped.

One popular feature is a seat cut into a thick hedge. If the hedge is really large, an arbour can even be created within it. A moon window, a round hole in the hedge through which you can see into the distance or into the next area of the garden, can bring a certain dynamism to a design. It is made simply by cutting

ABOVE Hedges do not have to be straight. All kinds of exciting shapes can be used. However, make certain that you cut tight to the shape each time or it will eventually be lost.

a hole in the hedge. This will look bare around the edges at first but with regularly trimming the inner surface eventually fills out to match the rest of the hedge. To keep the hole regular in shape, some gardeners insert a couple of metal hoops to act as formers.

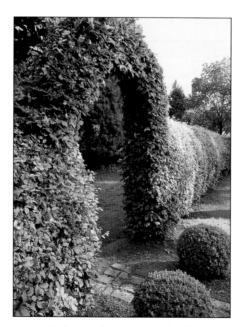

ABOVE Arches are important as they frame glimpses of what lies ahead. They can easily be formed in an existing hedge.

Arches

One of the most popular ways of articulating the top of a hedge is to create an arch. If the hedge is tall enough, this can be achieved simply by cutting through the hedge and creating an internal archway. On a lower hedge the arch must be created above the top line of the hedge. Essentially the arches are created in the same way. Cut a hole in the hedge to the required width. Leave the tops of the shrubs on either side of the proposed arch uncut and allow them to grow upwards. Gradually pull over the inner growth and tie together to form a rudimentary arch. As the main stems produce side shoots, trim these until eventually a solid top to the arch matching the hedge is formed. The "doorway" can be a sudden eruption in the line of the hedge, if the top is cut as a square or a semi-circle, or it can start some way down the hedge so that the line forms a gentle swell, more like a wave.

CREATING AN ARCH IN A HEDGE

Archways are not difficult to form in an existing hedge, although it will take several years for the arch to grow into its finished form. The main problem is to avoid accidentally cutting off the unkempt growth in the initial stages. Do not leave the shaping too long because it is easier to pull the shoots into shape while they are still young.

INITIAL PRUNING Any existing gap can be turned into an arch. Alternatively, a gap can be cut into the hedge but the inside faces will take several years to green over with leaves.

EARLY YEARS Leave up to three strong stems on each side of the hedge to grow vertically. Prune the rest of the hedge normally. At first the new growth will look a bit ragged.

SUBSEQUENT YEARS After one or two years, the shoots will be long enough to bend over to form the framework of the arch. If necessary, insert a wooden or metal framework to get the best shape.

ESTABLISHED PRUNING As the bent shoots fill out, trim them back so that they bush out, eventually creating the shape that you want. Once established, it can be trimmed as normal along with the hedge.

ABOVE An archway that has been gradually developed by allowing branches to grow tall and then training over a metal former.

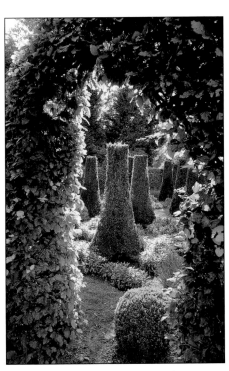

ABOVE A beech archway has the advantage that it holds on to its dead leaves throughout the winter, so its shape is still defined.

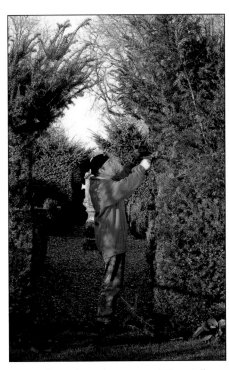

ABOVE An archway in progress. When tall enough the branches will be pulled over the gap and tied together to form the basis of the arch.

Renovating hedges

Over a period of time, or through lack of attention, many hedges become overgrown, and there comes a point when you have to bite the bullet and reduce it to near its original size. Such renovation is a rather daunting task but it can usually be successfully achieved.

Types of hedging

Not all hedging plants respond well to hard pruning. Yew (*Taxus*), holly (*Ilex*), hawthorn (*Crataegus*), beech (*Fagus*) and hornbeam (*Carpinus*) can all be cut back hard and they will soon regrow. Nearly all conifers object to such treatment. They will not reshoot and can even die. An overgrown conifer hedge is usually best replaced.

Techniques

Tackle an overgrown hedge by treating one surface at a time. This leaves plenty of foliage on the uncut surfaces to provide food and energy to allow the cut branches to regenerate. You should be aware that cutting a hedge

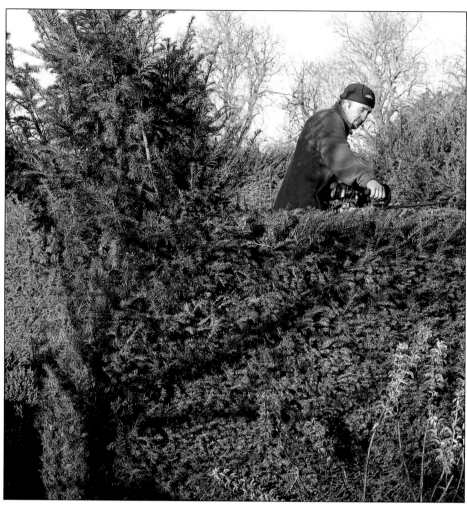

ABOVE Yew is one of the few conifers that can be really heavily cut back if it gets overgrown, without dying in the process.

RENOVATING AN OVERGROWN HEDGE

1 It is possible to reduce the width and height of an old hedge by drastic pruning over a couple of seasons. Tackle one side the first year and the other side the following year.

2 Use a pruning saw for the thick shoots at the centre of the hedge. However, you can use secateurs (pruners) or long-handled pruners on shoots that are thin enough.

3 New growth should appear from the stumps. Trim this growth back when it is about 15cm (6in) long to encourage bushy growth, then gradually allow it to reach the desired width.

HOW TO RENOVATE A HEDGE

An overgrown hedge can look a daunting task, but with the exception of some conifers it is not a difficult one. However, the process does take several years to complete and the hedge can look scruffy until it has filled out once again. Do not try to avoid this by cutting all the sides at once, as this may kill the hedge and will certainly slow it down.

YEAR ONE Start by dealing with one side of the hedge only. Cut it back to just inside the line that will form the new surface.

YEAR TWO OR THREE Once the hedge starts to grow back, cut the other side in a similar way. Cut the top of the hedge the following year.

hard back will result in an ugly appearance for at least the first year, but after that it will gradually fill out and will eventually look better for the harsh treatment.

First year

Cut back one face of the hedge. Reduce it to approximately 15cm (6in) shorter than the desired finished surface so that there is space for it to thicken out sufficiently. Try to make the face as flat as possible. If any of the branches are too thick to cut with shears or hedge trimmers, substitute secateurs and/or long-handled pruners. For really thick branches, a saw may be necessary. The other faces of the hedge should be trimmed only lightly, as normal.

Second and subsequent years

Leave a whole year before tackling the next face and then repeat the process, cutting back the second side heavily to up to 15cm (6in) below the final surface. Cut the top as normal and trim over the face you cut hard the previous year to ensure that the growth is even. This will also help to thicken the growth. Allow another year to pass, then tackle the top. Cut back to just below the required height. In subsequent years, you may trim the hedge as normally recommended for the type of plant.

Laying a hedge

Hedge-laying is a specialist task, but some gardeners tackle it successfully

ABOVE Laying a hedge is an art, but everyone has to start somewhere and it is possible for the gardener to create a very acceptable one.

themselves. The technique is best suited to country hedges composed of hawthorn, blackthorn or a mixture. The crudest form involves simply cutting partway through the thick stems of an overgrown hedge and bending them over, laying them on top of one another and hammering stakes in to keep them in line. This produces a bushy, rather ragged hedge. A more attractive, stronger and better-grown hedge can be achieved by first driving in hazel or chestnut stakes at about 1m (3ft) intervals along the hedge. The more flexible stems are then partially cut through, bent over and woven between the stakes to make a neat, relatively narrow hedge. Any pieces sticking out that cannot be woven in are cut off. Further lengths of hazel are then woven along the top to prevent the laid growth springing back. The now near-horizontal stems will throw up new upright growth, which, when trimmed, will make a dense, impenetrable hedge.

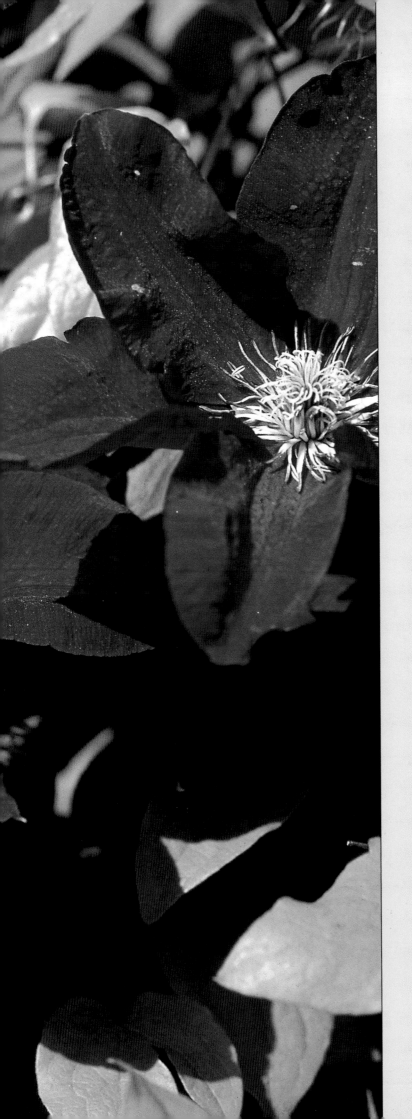

Ornamental Climbers and Wall Shrubs

Climbers and wall shrubs are important plants in gardens, providing height and structure, both around the margins of the garden on walls and fences, and also within the garden on poles, tripods or trellis. Not only do they provide colour and texture, they also create dappled shade when grown over pergolas or arbours. Climbers are also useful as screens both within the garden and around its margins.

Climbers and wall shrubs are generally very easy to grow. Some can be allowed to grow wild through trees, but the majority benefit from some pruning and training. They are no more difficult to prune than any other shrub. Nature is very forgiving and if you do make a few mistakes while you are learning, new growth will soon hide them. Use your common sense, knowledge of the plants and the information in this chapter.

LEFT One of the most popular ornamental climbers, clematis will produce a stunning display year after year, provided a few simple pruning rules are followed.

How climbers grow

How climbers grow is not something that many gardeners think about until they come to prune them, and then they begin to notice the differences. There are basically four types of climber, all with different methods of attaching themselves.

Twining plants

These attach themselves to host plants by means of their twining stems. Unpruned, they become a tangled mass of stems. A prime example of this group is honeysuckle (*Lonicera*). This embraces its host so tightly as to dig into it, leaving a distinct groove when removed. It can be difficult to remove dead or unwanted material on such climbers as it is often in the tight grip of newer wood.

Clinging plants

Some plants are equipped with modified roots that cling to surfaces like suckers. These, such as ivy (*Hedera*), are adapted to climb up tree trunks, cliff faces and rocks. In the garden, they provide useful cover on walls. However, they are often vigorous and can climb on to (even into) roofs, so have to be cut back regularly. When removed, they can leave dead roots stuck to the wall. If you need to paint a wall behind such a climber, it will have to be cut to the ground and allowed to start again.

Scrambling plants

The third category of climbing plants that needs to be mentioned is those that scramble up through other plants. They have no method of gripping the plant but rely on surrounding branches and twigs to support and hold them. Climbing roses and some clematis are in this category. Since they have no natural

ABOVE Some climbers are twiners. Hops and honeysuckle, for example, twine their way round their host.

ABOVE Climbers such as the climbing hydrangea have tiny aerial roots with which they attach themselves to walls.

ABOVE Some plants, such as rambling roses, scramble through or over other plants to reach the light.

DIFFERENT CLIMBING METHODS

The plants that we use as climbers in the ornamental garden are that which have adapted themselves to clamber up through other plants as well as up cliffs and over rocks in the wild so that they can expose their flowers to the light. In the garden, we create artificial hosts over which they can climb and scramble.

TWINING PLANTS (here hops and honeysuckle) Twining plants are best grown up vertical supports, such as poles, wires or trellising. They will also twine round other plants, although they may strangle them.

SCRAMBLING PLANTS (here clematis and roses) Scramblers are best grown through other plants, such as roses through a large tree. They can also be grown up various types of framework but will need tying in.

ABOVE Many clematis have tendrils (modified leaves) which they use to attach themselves to their host and their own stems.

way of holding on, they need to be tied into their support unless they are being allowed to climb through a shrub or tree. Even then, odd wayward shoots may need to be tied in. These types of climber need rather more attention, but if grown

against walls they can easily be removed for painting or other maintenance tasks, and then replaced. Most of the other categories of climber will also scramble up through shrubs and trees.

Plants with tendrils

This group of climbers, typified by many of the clematis, climbs through other plants by clinging on to them with tendrils. These are thin modified stems or leaves that twist into coils, gripping their host. Such plants can be self-supporting if given the right support, such as another plant or section of chicken netting. Odd stems can stray from the main plant and may need tying in.

Climbers that twine

Aconitum hemsleyanum
Actinidia (some)
Akebia
Ampelopsis
Fallopia
Humulus
Ipomoea
Jasminum (some)
Lonicera
Mandevilla
Phaseolus
Schizandra
Tropaeolum (some)
Wisteria

Climbers that cling

Decumaria barbara
Decumaria sinensis
Hedera canariensis
Hedera colchica
Hedera helix
Hydrangea anomala subsp. *petiolaris*
Parthenocissus henryana
Parthenocissus quinquefolia
Parthenocissus tricuspidata

Climbers that scramble

Akebia
Bignonia
Billardiera
Clematis (some)
Eccremocarpus
Euonymus (some)
Jasminum
Lapageria
Lathyrus (some)
Plumbago
Rhodochiton
Rosa (some)
Solanum (some)
Tropaeolum (some)
Vinca

Climbers with tendrils

Campsis radicans
Clematis (some)
Cobaea scandens
Lathyrus
Mutisia
Passiflora
Vitis

CLINGING PLANTS (here climbing hydrangea and boston ivy) Climbers that have their own aerial roots are best grown against a wall or fence. They can also be grown through trees, but can smother them.

PLANTS WITH TENDRILS (here sweet peas and clematis) Plants with tendrils wrap them round both the support and themselves. They are suitable for growing up trellises, wires, structures such as tripods, and other plants.

Support techniques

Climbers need some means of support. In the wild, this is provided by trees and shrubs or cliffs and rocks, but in the garden it is possible to choose a variety of supports to show off the plants to advantage.

Walls

Plants look good growing up walls. The walls show off the plants and the plants soften the shape of the walls. Self-clinging climbers will grow up walls without any further support, but all other types will need something to be tied in to. This can be wires, netting, trellis or special nails with lead heads that can be twisted around the branches.

Fences

Wire or netting fences look better clothed in climbers. Their structure is ideal for most climbers. Close-board fences and more solid structures need wires, netting or trellis fitted to them for the climbers to grip or be attached to. Check that all fences are strong enough to take the weight of the climber. Bear in mind that in wind the climber will add stress to the fence.

GROWING CLIMBERS ON WIRES

1 Wires should be firmly fixed to walls. One method uses screw eyes and involves drilling holes and using a plug of some sort.

2 Put the appropriate size plug in the hole and screw the eye well into the wall, leaving it sticking out by 3–5cm (1–2in).

3 Alternatively, a vine eye can be hammered into the wall. With hard walls, a pilot hole should be drilled first.

4 Use a strong wire and run it through the eyes of the support. Tension it as tightly as you can, then turn it back on itself and twist it.

5 Tie the climber or wall shrub in to the wire using a proprietary tie or some garden string.

6 As the climber or wall shrub continues to grow, tie in the shoots until the whole space is evenly covered.

Trellis

This is a framework of wood, or sometimes plastic, which can be used as a support for climbers on another feature, such as walls or fences, or in its own right, supported between poles. Trellis can be used on the boundaries of the garden as a fence or can be used internally to screen one part of the garden from another. The shape and design of the framework is irrelevant to the plants

GROWING CLIMBERS ON NETTING

1 Proprietary netting designed to be attached to walls and fences can be used to support climbers. Special clips are provided that screw or are nailed into the wall.

2 Carefully align the top two clips, using a spirit level, so that the netting will be straight.

3 Attach the netting to the top two clips.

4 With the netting held in place, align the other clips so that the netting is tight and straight, and then fasten them in place.

5 Train the climber up through the netting. Scramblers without any means of self support will need to be tied into position.

but can have a visual impact in the garden. A wide range of patterns is now available from garden centres and other sources. Many climbers will attach themselves to trellis, but some will need tying in.

Poles, tripods and obelisks

These methods of support all create a single climbing space for a climber, rather than a long line. Supports for climbers such as these make very pleasing decorative features in the garden. They can either be functional (for instance, three uprights inserted in the ground and tied at the top) or decorative in their own right (a carefully constructed and painted obelisk, for example). Poles should have netting attached to them in order to give the climbers something to grip on to. Tripods and obelisks may also need this, depending on how they are constructed.

GROWING CLIMBERS ON TRELLIS

1 An attractive support for a climber can be provided by using trellis. The trellis must be firmly fixed to a wall. Start by drilling a hole in the wall.

2 Screw a batten to the wall, rather than fixing the trellis directly to it. This will provide a gap behind the trellis.

3 Attach the trellis to the battens. It is a good idea to use hinges on the bottom batten and catches on the top one, so that it can be eased away from the wall for maintenance.

4 The firmly attached trellis is ready to support a climber or wall shrub. Most plants benefit from being tied in, even if they are self-clingers.

USING TRELLIS AS A SCREEN

1 Dig a hole in the position of the first post. It should be at least 45cm (18in) deep.

2 Place the post in the hole and make certain that it is vertical.

3 Fill the newly dug hole with a dry mix of concrete.

4 Dig the second hole one panel length away from the first post.

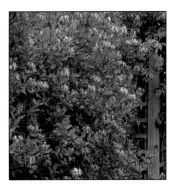

5 Attach the panel to the first post, using a hammer and nails, and then place the second post in its hole and attach the panel to that.

6 Make certain that the second post is upright and then fill in with a dry mix of concrete, ramming it down firmly.

7 Continue to add panels and posts until the trellis is finished. Until the concrete is set, the posts may need a brace to keep them upright.

ABOVE Honeysuckle in full bloom, covering trellis that has been used as a screen.

Arches, pergolas and arbours

Although their function is different, the construction of arches, pergolas and arbours is basically the same in that they all have sides and a top. Each may be made from wood or metal or can be constructed from panels of trellis. Many climbers will readily attach themselves to these structures and completely cover them (including the top), in the case of an arbour forming a green room. Wayward shoots should always be tied in, particularly thorny ones, as

ABOVE An archway with wisteria trained over it. Eventually, as it ages, it will be the wisteria holding up the arch.

they may catch on people walking through. When making these structures, always take into account the extent of the plants when fully grown. It is all too easy to make arches that will be too narrow when they are clothed with flourishing climbers.

Trees and shrubs

In the wild most climbers clamber up through trees and shrubs, and to a much lesser extent up cliffs and over rocks. In the garden, the latter is relatively rare but the former has all kinds of possibilities. One of the great advantages is that you can use climbers that flower at different times to the tree or shrub; thus the support might flower in spring and the climber in summer or late summer, making effective use of the space. There are some climbers, *Clematis viticella* and all its cultivars, for example, that are pruned back to the ground each spring, so that the shrubby support is uncluttered when it flowers but by the end of summer the climber has grown again and fills the shrub with flowers. It is important that any tree or shrub that is used as a support is in good health, as the extra weight of the climber, plus the windage its bulk

GROWING CLIMBERS UP TRIPODS

1 Place three poles into holes in the ground and refill the holes with earth, or concrete if it is an exposed site.

3 Saw off the ends flush with the uprights, and add the rest of the horizontal bars, making as many levels as you want.

5 Water the plant well and then mulch around it in order to preserve moisture and keep weeds down.

6 The finished tripod. A smaller one can be made by sloping three poles towards each other and tying or nailing them at the top.

2 Nail a cross bar between two of the poles using galvanized nails. Use overlong lengths to avoid splitting the wood.

4 Put the plant either in the centre or on one of the sides. Avoid the corners if these have been concreted.

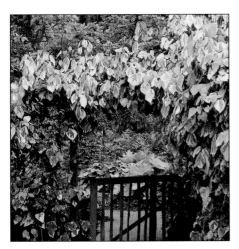

ABOVE Climbers can be trained over archways. Some, like this ivy, will soon find their own way over and need little tying in.

creates, can put a tremendous strain on the plant. It is dangerous to grow climbers through dead trees. It is not such a good idea to grow ivy through a tree because it will eventually smother it and is likely to kill it. Having said that, it is perfect for adding a decaying, gothic look to a garden.

BUILDING AN ARCH

1 Make sure that the arch is wide enough to include the width of the plants and still leave enough room to walk through it.

2 Dig the holes for the uprights in the appropriate places, preferably at least 45cm (18in) deep, but more if possible.

3 Make certain that the uprights are vertical and then concrete the arch in position. Cover the concrete with soil to disguise it.

4 Assemble the top of the archway on the ground, choosing a pitch that will look right. Experiment with temporary fixing if necessary.

5 Using galvanized nails, secure the top to the uprights, being careful not to knock the uprights out of the vertical.

GROWING CLIMBERS THROUGH SHRUBS

1 The shrub does not have to be large. Small shrubs can accommodate small climbers, such as *Clematis alpina*.

2 Prepare the ground beside, not under, the shrub, otherwise the climber might be starved of water.

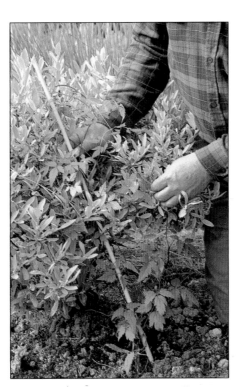

3 Plant the climber in the prepared soil and tie its shoots to one or more canes, leading them into the shrub.

4 Finally, water the newly planted climber thoroughly and apply a mulch to prevent the evaporation of moisture.

Initial training

Most climbing plants have a natural tendency to grow straight up. Some kind of training is essential if you want them to provide good coverage on a wall or trellis.

On receipt of the plant

Most plants that you buy from garden centres and nurseries need little initial pruning after planting. Remove or cut back any damaged shoots or any that are dead or diseased. (This applies mainly to plants dug up by friends. You would normally reject plants in this state for sale in nurseries.) Any weak shoots should also be cut off. Most climbers are sold in pots, but occasionally they may be bare-rooted. If you have not got the time to plant these immediately, they should be heeled in in some spare ground.

After planting

The plant should be set close to its support. However, if planting against a wall or fence, site it at least 25cm (10in) away, preferably more. Check the stems again and cut out any that have been damaged during

ABOVE The rose 'Albertine' trained on wires on the tiled side of a garage. It is important to tie in all the shoots. You will also need to ensure that the rose does not grow into the eaves.

transportation or planting. Train the shoots towards the support. If this is a wall or fence, place several canes at an angle between it and the plant. Tie the shoots to these. If they are long enough, start training them up the wall by tying into the support. When planting against trellis or poles, the plants are usually close enough to train the shoots directly on to the supports. In both cases, even twining plants are best tied in

to start with, although they will soon start finding their own way of clinging to the support.

With most forms of support, it is important to ensure that the initial training separates the various shoots, so that the climber is well spread across the wall or trellis rather than concentrated in a tangled column up its centre. With some of the more woody climbers, such as roses, it is a good idea to arch the stems so that

TRAINING A CLIMBER AGAINST A FENCE

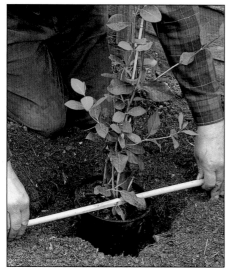

1 Prepare a planting hole and check that it is the correct depth. Most plants need to be at the same depth as they were in the pot.

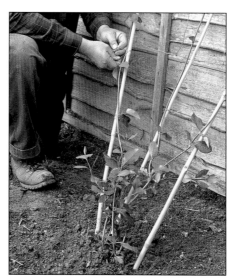

2 Put the plant in the hole and then train the shoots to their support, spreading them as widely as possible to give a good coverage.

3 Once planted, water thoroughly and then apply a mulch to prevent evaporation and help keep weeds down.

ABOVE Climbers, particularly annuals, are suitable for growing in containers. Various supports are available.

the tips are almost as low as their origin. This will encourage them to produce more shoots along their length, ensuring good coverage of the wall or whatever support you are using. You should also separate out the stems of plants climbing up a single pole, for even coverage.

As the plant grows, tie in any shoots that are beginning to wave free from the support. Even self-twining plants need tying in from time to time. If possible, direct some of the shoots to fill spaces so that eventually the whole wall or support is covered.

ABOVE A collection of different types of proprietary plastic plant ties and string. Ties are quick but string is cheaper.

DIFFERENT TRAINING METHODS

The basic principle of training climbers is to ensure that the plant covers as much as possible of its allotted space. The simpler the system of training that you use, the easier it is to prune the climber. Tangled shoots can take a lot of time to sort out. Below is a selection of methods for training ornamental climbers.

TRAINING AGAINST TRELLIS When planting against a piece of trellis, spread out the bottom shoots as widely as possible, the outside ones preferably horizontally so that a curtain of foliage is created.

A BADLY TRAINED CLIMBER ON TRELLIS When training up a trellis, make sure that the stems are well spread out at the base, so that they cover the whole of the allotted space rather than, as here, forming a tight column.

TRAINING AGAINST A WALL The same principle applies to a wall as to a trellis. Spread out the shoots as widely as possible so that the space is clothed all the way from the ground.

TRAINING OVER AN ARCH Plant on the outside of archways so that the passageway is not constricted by the growing plant. Train the shoots right over the top of the arch, keeping an even spread.

Established pruning

In many ways the principles involved in pruning climbers are the same as for other forms of ornamental shrub. The only basic difference is that you are dealing with long, vertical stems and pruning may involve using ladders or platforms.

ABOVE It is essential to cut back wall climbers when they reach the line of the gutter to stop them getting under the tiles and eaves.

Routine pruning

Pruning established climbers can appear daunting. Start by cutting out any dead, damaged or diseased wood. In the case of a tangled climber, such as a mature *Clematis montana*, there may be a mass of dead material within it. Next remove any weak or unproductive growth. Also cut back any crossing stems or stems that are causing congestion. Finally, look for some of the older stems and cut these back hard, either to strong new growth or completely to the ground. This will stimulate new growth, which will keep the climber healthy and productive. The best time to do this varies but winter is often a good time on a deciduous climber as it is easy to gain access to the base of the plant.

Summer pruning

Some climbers flower on the previous year's wood. These should be pruned in summer, as soon as the plant has finished flowering. This promotes new growth, which will ripen in time to produce the following year's flowers.

Arched stems

All new wood should be trained as it grows. With climbers such as honeysuckle, tie in the new growth to fill gaps and provide an even spread. With woodier subjects such

PRUNING AN ESTABLISHED CLIMBER

1 A honeysuckle growing over a pergola. This climber is becoming overgrown and is in need of pruning.

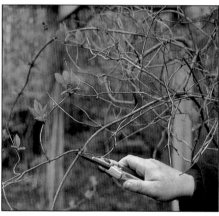

2 The first task when pruning is to remove all the dead and damaged wood. Honeysuckle often has a lot of the former.

3 Cut the dead wood back to the next healthy shoot or, if congested, take it back even further, but always to a shoot.

4 The next task is to cut out some of the congested wood, preferably taking out the weakest and oldest growth.

5 Select some of the strongest and most healthy growths to be retained. These are likely to be the youngest wood.

6 Tie these healthy shoots in to the post or pillar or the cross members of the pergola, using garden string.

PRUNING ESTABLISHED CLIMBERS

The pruning of established climbers is often ignored, mainly because it involves working with a ladder. It can also be difficult, but it is essential that ornamental climbers are just as well maintained as any other shrubs in the garden. Some climbers need quite a lot of work in order to keep them at their best, while others just need trimming round the edges.

AN ESTABLISHED CLIMBER Take out any dead or damaged wood. Remove any congested wood and then take out a few of the oldest stems back to a good shoot. This will promote rejuvenation.

EAVES AND GUTTERS You will need to stop many self-clinging wall climbers getting into gutters and obscuring windows.

as roses, the new wood should be trained, as far as possible, in a horizontal curve. This not only promotes flowering along the whole branch, but also stimulates new shoots, which can also be trained in a curve, so that the wall is covered when the climber is in full bloom. Tie the stems vertically and they will flower only at the top. To achieve this, there are some climbers, such as roses, where you will have to take the climber off the wall, spread it on the ground, prune it and then put it back, tying the stems into nice curving arcs. Fortunately, it is not necessary to do this every year.

Gutters and roofs

While the aim is to cover as much of a wall with a climber as possible, it is not advisable to let them extend above the gutter level. Many climbers, and in particular self-clinging ones, will find any gap and penetrate the roof-space of the building. They can even go up under the eaves and squeeze in between tiles. They can also clog up gutters, not only with their stems but also with their fallen leaves. Make certain, therefore, that they do not reach this height. Every autumn, cut back any shoots that have ventured above the top of the wall. It is a good idea to cut them back by at least 30cm (12in), so that they will not immediately grow back the following spring. Do the job in autumn rather than spring, as you will then be able to clear the stems and leaves from the gutters before the winter rains.

On houses and other buildings, it is also important to ensure that the climbers are kept back from windows, and, in the case of self-clingers such as ivy, from any woodwork that is regularly painted.

ABOVE To rejuvenate a climber, cut back some of the older wood to a strong shoot.

ABOVE Wood that is dead or contains die-back, as here, should be cut back to a good shoot.

Clematis group I

Clematis are normally divided into three groups as far as pruning is concerned. The grouping reflects their time of flowering and the best way to prune them to achieve the maximum number of flowers. Group I consists of those that flower on the previous season's wood and so require little or no pruning (or the flowering wood will be removed). The typical clematis in this group is *Clematis montana* and its cultivars. Several other species also fall into this category.

Initial pruning and training

Plant the clematis deeper in the soil than it was in the pot. The pot soil line should be about 5cm (2in) or more below the level of the ground. This is to ensure that if the plant suffers from clematis wilt, there will be some adventitious buds that will throw up new shoots and so ensure the plant's survival. Little initial pruning is then required other than to remove any damaged wood. You also need to make sure that the shoots are well spread out

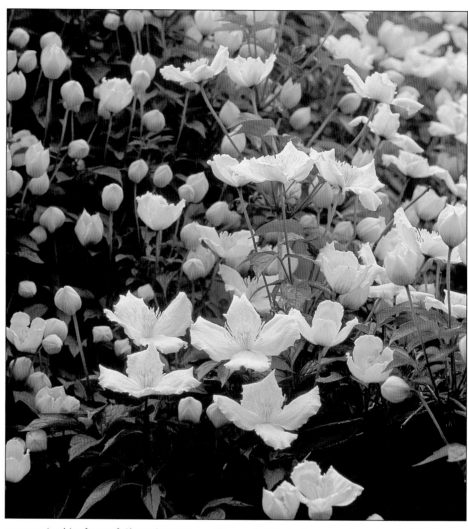

ABOVE A white form of *Clematis montana*. This needs little in the way of pruning, but if it is left unattended it can become rather congested.

PRUNING CLEMATIS GROUP 1

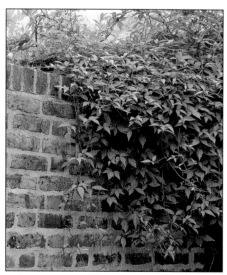

1 Clematis in this group can largely be left to their own devices in terms of pruning, but some, especially *C. montana*, can get very congested and over-heavy.

2 Little new growth on this clematis needs to be removed, except for a few straggly growths or where the climber is starting to outgrow its position.

3 The surface of the climber looks almost the same, but beneath it is likely to be a tangle of dead wood, which will need removing.

ABOVE When pruning clematis, find a pair of strong shoots and cut across the stem just above, being careful not to damage them.

and tie any new ones in to a fan shape so that the whole of the support will be covered.

Established pruning

This is the easiest clematis group in that theoretically no pruning is required, as the flowers are formed on the previous year's wood. However, it is prudent to cut out any dead wood, as this can quickly build up, especially on *C. montana*. This accumulation of dead wood will not only stifle the clematis, making it look like a vast bird's nest, but it will also create a tremendous weight that may well bring down the support. So, at least every couple of years, go through the climber and take out any dead wood you can find – a tedious job but worth doing. If the clematis grows beyond its bounds, there is no harm in

HOW TO PRUNE CLEMATIS GROUP 1 In this group the flowers are formed on the previous year's wood, so a harsh pruning will remove these and hence its ability to flower in the current year. This group needs very little pruning other than that required to keep the plant under control and to remove any dead wood that may accumulate. The latter will tend to build up, making the plant very congested.

Group 1 clematis

All the cultivars of the various species below also belong to Group 1.

C. alpina
C. armandii
C. cirrhosa
C. macropetala
C. montana

cutting off the offending shoots at any time of the year as long as you cut back to a strong bud.

Renovation

C. montana, in particular, can become very overgrown and full of dead wood if it is not regularly maintained. At some point, you will inevitably have to prune it severely to bring it back under control, which is a satisfying task. Fortunately, *C. montana* can be cut back very hard and will still rejuvenate, so after taking out all the dead wood, cut back into the older wood, leaving some of the younger shoots. If extreme action is called for you can cut it back almost to the ground. All this should take place immediately after flowering.

Clematis group 2

The second group of clematis includes most of the large-flowered varieties, including 'Lasurstern' and 'Nelly Moser'. These tend to have two flowerings, the main crop in the early summer on the previous year's wood and then a second crop on the new wood in late summer or autumn.

Initial training

Ensure that the young clematis is planted deeper in the soil than it was in the pot. Make sure that the pot soil line is about 5cm (2in) or more below ground level. This is to ensure that there will be some adventitious buds that will throw up new shoots and so ensure the plant's survival if the plant suffers from clematis wilt. You should find that little initial pruning is required other than to remove any damaged wood, although many gardeners like to cut back all stems to a pair of strong buds about 30cm (12in) or so above the ground. Also ensure that the shoots are well spread out and tie any new ones in to a fan shape so that the whole of the support will be covered.

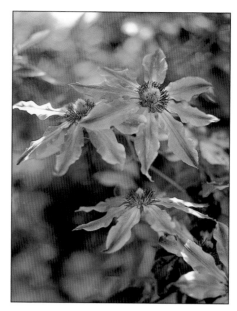

ABOVE *Clematis* 'Barbara Dibley' is typical of the large-flowered varieties that belong to this group of clematis.

Established pruning

This is the most complicated of the clematis groups, although once you have done it a few times, it presents no problems. It is also reassuring to know that even if you cut something off that you didn't mean to, it doesn't really matter as the plant will tolerate being cut hard back. Pruning takes place in late winter, before the

ABOVE The double *Clematis* 'Royalty'. Group 2 clematis need a little more attention than those in the other two groups.

growth really gets under way (some growth may even have started by mid-winter, but do not worry about this, even if it gets cut off).

Firstly, remove any dead, dying or diseased wood. Next, cut back all the remaining shoots to the first pair of strong buds, which can be at varying points on the stems. In some cases, you will remove only a short length

PRUNING CLEMATIS GROUP 2

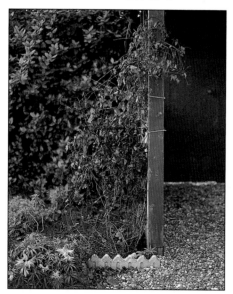

1 The clematis in early spring looks very difficult to prune, but it is not quite as bad as it appears.

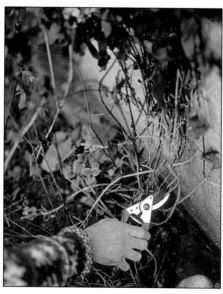

2 Start by removing a few of the older shoots back to a pair of buds at the base, so that the plant is constantly rejuvenated.

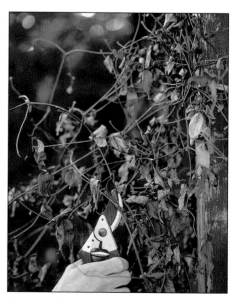

3 Next cut back all the remaining stems to the topmost pair of strong buds. If necessary, retie all the shoots, spreading them out if possible.

ABOVE 'Lasurstern' is a Group 2 clematis. The large purple flowers make a wonderful feature in the garden.

but in others you may cut back half the stem. Look carefully at the remaining structure and retie any shoots that may be better used to fill gaps, so that you achieve as even a spread as possible.

Renovation

If the clematis becomes neglected or simply overgrown, you can cut it back quite severely and it will generally recover. If you are a little uncertain, reduce the plant by a third every year until it has all been renewed.

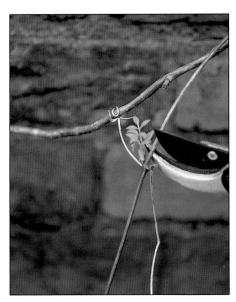

ABOVE The best time to prune is late winter before growth starts, but this may have started by then so do not damage new shoots.

HOW TO PRUNE CLEMATIS GROUP 2 This group can be left unpruned but the flowering wood would get higher and higher, as well as more congested, so it is better to prune lightly to keep them under control. Take the opportunity to retie shoots to fill gaps and relieve congestion. Take back the shoots to the topmost pair of strong buds. Any dead or damaged wood should also be removed and one or two of the oldest stems can be removed almost to the base to rejuvenate the clematis.

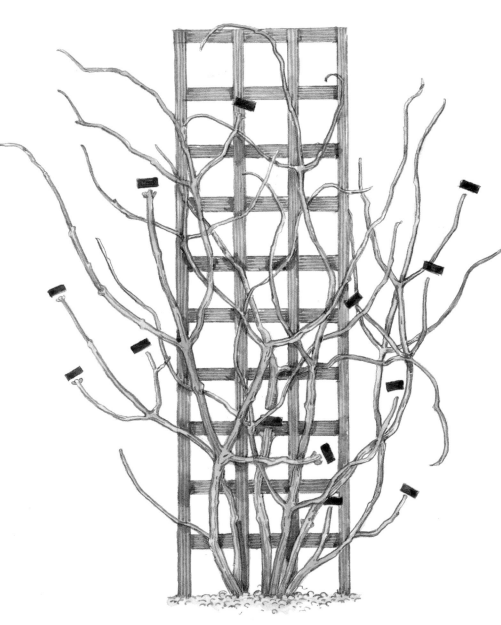

Group 2 clematis

C. 'Barbara Dibley'	C. 'Elsa Späth'	C. 'Moonlight'
C. 'Barbara Jackman'	C. 'Fireworks'	C. 'Nelly Moser'
C. 'Belle of Woking'	C. 'H.F. Young'	C. 'Proteus'
C. 'Countess of Lovelace'	C. 'Lasurstern'	C. 'Star of India'
C. 'Daniel Deronda'	C. 'Marie Boisselot'	C. 'The President'
C. 'Dr Ruppel'	C. 'Miss Bateman'	C. 'Vyvyan Pennell'

Clematis group 3

The third group is another easy group to deal with. It is typified by *C. viticella* and its host of cultivars. These are mainly the smaller-flowered varieties, which tend to produce their blooms in late summer and into autumn, on the current year's wood. If they are left unpruned, the climbers get taller and taller and the flowers appear right at the top, leaving an unsightly mass of tangled brown stems at eye-level. They are ideal for growing through other shrubs such as roses. At the beginning of the summer, the clematis is not far into the bush so the roses can be clearly seen, but by late summer, when the roses have finished, the clematis is in full flower, giving the shrub a second flush of life.

Initial training

When planting the young clematis, check that it is planted deeper in the soil that it was in the pot. You will

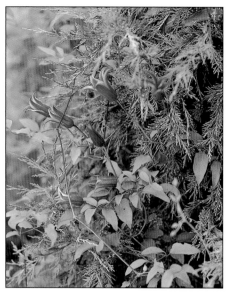

ABOVE Group 3 are good for growing through other shrubs as, being cut to the ground each year, they do not swamp their host.

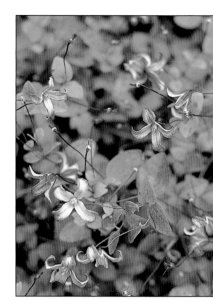

ABOVE All the *viticella* group of clematis belong to Group 3, and are pruned in the same way. These include 'Pagoda', seen here.

need to have the pot soil line about 5cm (2in) or more below the level of the ground. The reason for this is to ensure that if the plant suffers from clematis wilt, there will be some adventitious buds that will throw up new shoots and so ensure

the plant's survival. On planting, cut back all stems to a pair of strong buds about 30cm (12in) or so above the ground. As the new shoots develop, ensure that they are well spread out and tie them in so that the whole of the support will be covered.

ABOVE The tangled wood resulting from one year's growth. Fortunately, there is no need to sort it all out – it can all be cut off.

PRUNING CLEMATIS GROUP 3

1 The main pruning technique with this group is to cut all the stems back to a bud or new shoot close to the base of the plant.

2 Any remaining dead or damaged wood should be cut right back to the base. There will always be a few such shoots.

Group 3 clematis

C. 'Abundance'	C. 'Fair Rosamund'	C. 'Star of India'
C. 'Ascotiensis'	C. 'Lady Betty Balfour'	C. tangutica
C. 'Bill Mackenzie'	C. 'Little Nell'	C. tibetana (orientalis)
C. 'Comtesse de Bouchard'	C. 'Madame Julia Correvon'	C. viticella and cvs
C. 'Duchess of Albany'	C. 'Perle d'Azur'	
C. 'Etoile Violette'	C. 'Royal Velours'	

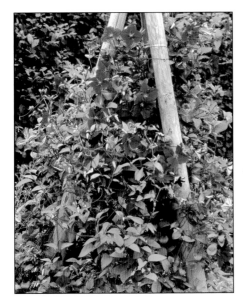

ABOVE An impressive amount of growth is put on during one season and the plant gathers strength each year; it will soon cover this tripod.

Established pruning

In late winter, cut back all stems to the first strong pair of buds above the point where you cut them last year. Pull all the old growth from the supports. There will probably be some growth starting towards the tips of the old growth, but do not be afraid to cut this off. The plant will soon burst into life from the base.

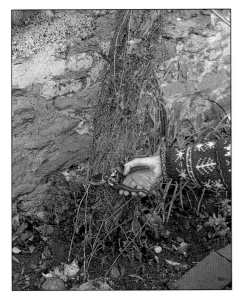

ABOVE Do not cut the shoots too high, especially when they are young, or they will gradually get taller as the years go by, leaving the base bare.

HOW TO PRUNE CLEMATIS GROUP 3 The group 3 clematis are very easy to deal with, which can be a relief because the previous year's growth always looks a tangled mess. Pruning is best done in late winter and regrowth will start almost immediately. Cut all the stems back to the first pair of strong buds above where you cut the previous year. Cut out any dead stems completely. As the new stems grow, weave or tie them in as necessary.

Unusual clematis

There is a small group of clematis that can be pruned either as Group 2 or Group 3. Treated as Group 2, they will flower earlier with larger flowers. As Group 3 they will flower later (which can be an advantage), but with smaller flowers.

C. 'Duchess of Sutherland'
C. 'Ernest Markham'

C. 'Gipsy Queen'
C. 'Hagley Hybrid'
C. 'Jackmanii'
C. 'Jackmanii Superba'
C. 'Maureen'
C. 'Mrs Cholmondeley'
C. 'Niobe'
C. 'Rouge Cardinal'
C. 'Ville de Lyon'
C. 'W.E. Gladstone'

Wisteria

Pruning wisteria causes most gardeners more anguish than any other climber. In fact, it is a simple matter and all you need to remember is that wisteria needs pruning twice a year, instead of once a year as with most other climbers.

Supports

Although wisteria can be trained as a standard tree, it is most commonly seen as a wall climber. It cannot cling to the wall by itself like ivy, so needs a support. Its sheer size means that wooden trellis is usually out of the question. It is best supported on a series of parallel wires fixed securely to the wall with vine eyes. The wires should be about 30cm (12in) apart, with the bottom one about 60cm (2ft) from the ground, or higher if you wish. Put a stake into the ground to support the main stem for the first couple of years.

Initial training

Plant in winter or early spring. Cut back the leader to about 1m (3ft) above the ground and remove all side shoots. During the summer, choose two well-placed laterals and tie them into the wires at an angle of 45 degrees. Cut back any side shoots on these to three or four buds. Remove all other laterals. Tie the leader in a

ABOVE Wisteria can create a wonderful walkway when trained over a pergola. The main stems twine their way up and across the poles.

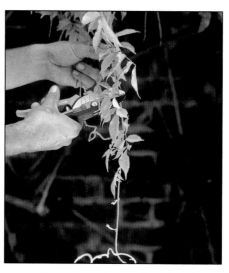

ABOVE Summer pruning consists of cutting back the shoots to within five or six leaves of the new growth. Shorten this again in winter.

vertical position. During its second winter, remove about one-third of the length of the laterals and gently pull them down to the horizontal. Cut the leader off at about 75–90cm (30–36in) above the top lateral. The following summer repeat the process of the first summer and tie in two good new laterals at an angle of 45 degrees. Remove all other new laterals. Tie down to the horizontal in winter and cut back the top third of each lateral, including the two trained the previous year. Cut back all side shoots to three or four buds. Continue in the same vein until the wisteria covers the whole wall.

Established pruning

Once established, continue to prune wisteria in both summer and winter. In late summer, prune each lateral and side shoot to within about five or six leaves from the main lateral. Allow the main lateral to develop until it has filled its space. Once this has happened, cut back annually to five or six leaves of the new growth. In winter, return to the same shoots and reduce them further to two or three buds. If you do this every year, the wisteria should not become overgrown. If it does, remove one main branch each year over several years, allowing a suitable replacement to develop.

ABOVE Wisterias are ideal for training on to walls, which help to protect the young buds from late frosts.

ABOVE The shoots that are not required for extending the wisteria's coverage should be cut back to two or three buds in winter.

TRAINING A WISTERIA

Wisteria is often thought by many gardeners to be a difficult plant to train and prune. This is mainly because the task needs to be done twice a year, once in the summer and then again in the winter. However, the actual pruning process is not at all difficult and should soon become a matter of routine, although it might involve some ladder work.

YEAR ONE, WINTER Plant the wisteria in winter or early spring. Cut back all the side shoots and cut back the leader to about 1m (36in).

YEAR ONE, SUMMER In the following summer, select two strong shoots and tie these into the wires. Also tie in the vertical leader. Remove all other laterals.

YEAR TWO, WINTER In the second winter, gently pull the two laterals down to the horizontal. Cut off the leader about 75–90cm (30–36in) above the laterals.

YEAR TWO, SUMMER The following summer, repeat the process that you completed in the previous year, this time adding a second tier of new laterals.

YEAR THREE, WINTER Again, repeat what you did in the previous winter and continue until the space is covered with horizontal branches, which will form the framework.

ESTABLISHED PRUNING, SUMMER Once the wisteria is established, prune any new shoots that are not required to fill a space back to five or six leaves of the new growth.

ESTABLISHED PRUNING, WINTER Each winter cut back all the shoots pruned in the summer to two or three buds. Cut out completely any shoots that cross or cause congestion.

Renovation pruning

With controlled pruning every year, plants should never become overgrown and need a complete overhaul. However, sometimes pruning is forgotten or put off until such time as it is too late. And you often inherit shrubs and climbers that have been allowed to run riot.

Making a start

There are some cases where you can literally chop the plants off close to the ground and start again, but generally a more controlled approach is required. Furthermore, in some cases it may be possible to carry out the renovation in one year, but in other cases it may take several years to renovate the plant completely. So before you start, it is important establish what kind of plant you have. An ancient wisteria may be permanently fixed to a wall, but there are some climbers, roses for example, that can gradually be untied and lowered to the ground for pruning before being returned to the support. This is a good opportunity to check all the supports to make sure they are in good condition, with none of the wires corroded or likely to snap. If the wall or support is painted, this may also be the time to give it a couple of fresh coats.

Pruning

First, cut out all the dead wood along with anything that is damaged or diseased. This allows you to see

RENOVATING A CLIMBER

1 Once climbers become a tangled mess, they will need a complete overhaul. It is often easier to untie the climber from its support in order to carry out the work.

2 The best place to start is to take out all the dead or damaged wood. This clears out quite a lot of unwanted material, making it easier to see where to go next.

3 Next, cut out some of the thin and congested wood to open up the structure. Quite a lot of wood can be removed at this stage of the renovation process.

4 Take out some of the older wood right back to a bud just above the soil, so that the plant rejuvenates from the base.

5 Start to tie back some of the remaining shoots, spreading them evenly across the space and trying to fill in any gaps.

6 The renovation is almost completed. There are still a number of weak shoots that remain and these should be taken out as well.

HOW TO RENOVATE CLIMBERS

If at all possible, you should attempt to keep the climbers in your garden under control. However, you will inevitably find that occasionally they get unruly, or you may be taking over a garden that has an array of congested, overgrown plants.

Some climbers do not like being pruned too hard, so spread the hard pruning over two or more years for these.

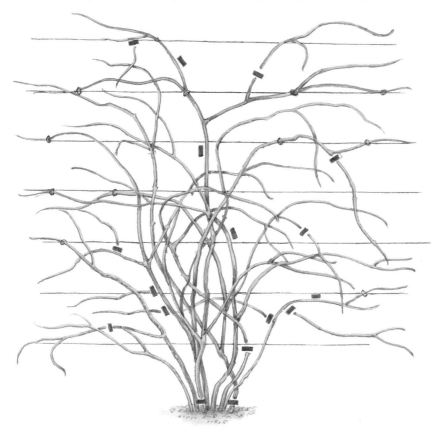

BASIC RENOVATION Cut out any dead or damaged wood and then turn your attention to taking out weak growth along with any branches or stems that cross or cause congestion. Finally take out some of the older wood completely.

CUTTING HARD BACK There are some climbers, such as honeysuckle, that can be pruned back very hard, taking them almost to the base.

Aftercare

Prune all new wood every year in the normal way, so that the climber does not need renovating again. Tie in all new growths as they appear. To encourage new growth, top-dress the area around the base of the climber with a general fertilizer, then water and mulch.

the framework of the living climber. After this, remove any weak, spindly growth, cutting back either to a main branch or to a good strong shoot. Any crossing or rubbing wood can now be removed. At this point, look at what you have got left and, if you feel that to remove any more may damage the plant, leave it until next winter. However, if possible, remove at least one main stem of older wood. Usually this can be cut back right to the base. It may be possible to take out two. By the following year, new growth should have replaced these. Gradually, over the next two or three years, take out all the old growth, so that you are left with a vigorous new plant.

ABOVE Summer reveals the recovered plant. Here, the right-hand side needs some stems trained horizontally, as on the left.

Wall shrubs

There are certain shrubs that, while not strictly climbers, look good when trained against walls. Chaenomeles, for example, will grow perfectly happily as a free-standing shrub, but has a loose and sparsely flowering habit. When trained tight against a wall, it comes into its own and will often flower profusely for many weeks.

Supports

Although most of the wall shrubs can be grown as free-standing plants, they still require support when grown against a wall. This is not only to give them strength in their unnatural position, but also to prevent the wind bouncing off the wall behind and blowing them forward. They also tend to reach forwards towards the light. It is possible to attach some form of trellis or heavy netting, either wood, metal or plastic, to the wall. This can be very effective in small quantities, and if hinged at the bottom, the plant can be eased away from the wall for painting and maintenance, as required. However, to cover larger areas of wall and for a more discreet look, parallel wires anchored to the wall with vine eyes are better. The wires should not be tight against the wall but should be held at least 5cm (2in) away from it.

Initial training

Plant the shrub at least 30cm (12in) away from the wall, preferably more. The soil is often poorer close to a wall and is usually too dry. When the shrub is fully grown the fact that it is not planted tight to the wall will not be apparent. On planting, some method may be needed to attach the shrub to the wall. If the main shoot or shoots are long enough, they can be tied directly to the lower wires,

PRUNING FREMONTODENDRON

1 Fremontodendron is coated with a dust that can cause problems if it is inhaled, so wear a mask and goggles when pruning.

2 As with most pruning jobs, the first routine task is to cut out all the dead, diseased or damaged wood.

3 Not much else is required, except to remove any misplaced shoots. Tie the remaining shoots into the framework.

4 Use string or a proprietary plant tie for tying in. Fremontodrendons are best trained as a fan or an espalier.

but in many cases it will be necessary first to tie the shoots to a cane or canes that are angled towards the wall.

The main way of training depends on the shrub and its natural habit. Some can be trained with a central "trunk", with branches spreading to

either side of it, while others are best as fans. For a less formal look, simply tie in main branches as they develop and cut out any shoots that project from or grow towards the wall. This usually works well as long as you also cut out any crossing or congested wood, and tie in odd shoots into gaps to produce even coverage over the wall.

A more formal way is to train a shrub as a fan or even as an espalier in the same way as you would a fruit tree. For a fan, start with two strong laterals at the bottom and tie these in at an angle of 35 degrees. Allow other sub-laterals to develop on these and tie them in at an angle until the whole wall space is covered. Chaenomeles responds well to this training. For an espalier, allow two laterals to develop and tie them in to horizontal wires. Allow the main leaders to grow and produce two more laterals the following year. Train these sideways and so on until all the wires have horizontal arms on them. A suitable subject for this training is *Fremontodendron*.

Established training

Apply the same principles as you would to a free-standing shrub. Also, remove all shoots that grow towards the wall or away from it, and make certain that there are no crossing or rubbing shoots. If areas become bare (perhaps because of the need to cut out dead or damaged wood), train new shoots to cover the spot.

WALL-TRAINING AN ESPALIERED PYRACANTHA Pyracantha is a classic wall shrub. It can be trained flat against a wall, rather than letting it bush out into a more shrub-like shape in the open garden. Pyracantha has rather vicious spines, so it is advisable to wear gloves when pruning it. For a more formal-looking pyracantha, the initial training could shape the plant into an espalier with decorative tiers of horizontal branches. Cut out all of the wood that points away from the wall, and so spoils the effect.

PRUNING A WALL-TRAINED PYRACANTHA

1 Most of the pruning is carried out in the summer. Cut back shoots to just a couple of buds to prevent the bush from becoming too dense, and to expose the fruit.

2 Cut back shoots that are growing away from the wall to one bud or, if the area is already well supplied with shoots, take them out completely.

3 A young pyracantha still in the process of filling out. This has been trained into an espalier shape, but it could also be trained as a fan.

Pruning ceanothus

Evergreen ceanothus not only look good against walls but, especially in cooler areas, also appreciate the protection a wall provides. They do not respond well to hard pruning.

Supports

Either use wires or a section of trellis attached to a wall as a support. Trellis provides more points at which to anchor the stems. Once the shrub has grown, it will hardly be seen.

Initial training

Allow the shrub to develop in its natural way, but remove all shoots that grow either towards or away from the wall. Also take out any shoots that cross over others or cause congestion. Aim for even coverage across the allotted space. Do not cut back into old wood to try to stimulate growth.

Established pruning

Evergreen ceanothus flower either on the previous year's wood or on the current year's wood. They are very reluctant to break again from old wood, so all that is required, beyond removing any dead, damaged or diseased wood, is to tip-prune the previous year's shoots back to one bud in early spring. This will produce flowering shoots and maintain the shrub's shape and size. Old overgrown ceanothus should be dug out.

WALL-TRAINING A CEANOTHUS There are two distinct types of ceanothus: the evergreen and the deciduous. It is important to keep control of the shape if you use a ceanothus as a wall shrub, because it is difficult to cut back if it becomes overgrown. Train the shrub to be relatively flat against the wall, cutting back any shoots that stick too far out from the wall. Then, lightly tip-prune the previous year's growth if the shrub is likely to get too large.

ABOVE The flowers of evergreen ceanothus appear on the previous year's wood, so do not cut it back unless you need to.

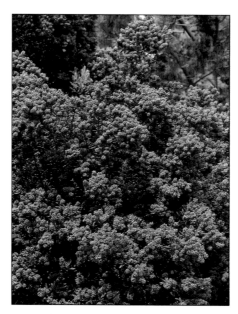

ABOVE If ceanothus is grown as a freestanding bush, there is little pruning required. It can be allowed to grow naturally, the only pruning being the removal of dead wood.

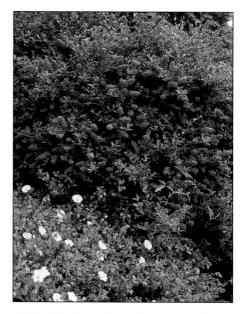

ABOVE This clearly shows the new shoots developing, which will carry next year's flowers. If it is necessary to control the plant, they must be pruned only lightly.

Pruning chaenomeles

Chaenomeles makes a superb wall shrub. The aim is to keep it cut back tight to the wall. Some varieties will flower throughout the year, often profusely.

Support

This is best supported on a system of parallel wires, at about 30cm (12in) intervals.

Initial training

There are two ways to train a chaenomeles against a wall. The more professional way is to create a fan, much in the same way as for a fruit fan. Plant a young specimen and cut off the leader immediately above the top one of two strong laterals. Tie these in at an angle of about 30 degrees and remove all other laterals. Cut out their tips to about 45cm (18in) from the main trunk. Allow these to develop two side shoots each and tie these in. Remove the tips of the side shoots in a similar fashion and reduce all other side shoots to one bud. Continue doing this each year until the whole space is covered with an evenly spaced framework of stems. Alternatively, allow the shrub to

FAN-TRAINING A CHAENOMELES Chaenomeles can be grown as a free-standing shrub in the garden, but is most commonly seen grown as a wall shrub, where it should be kept tightly pruned. The best way in which to train a chaenomeles is as a fan against a wall or fence, allowing the stems to branch until the whole space is evenly covered.

develop naturally, tying in the main six or seven side shoots as they appear, so that the area is well covered. Allow these to produce side shoots in order to fill in the gaps. Cut off any shoots pointing towards or away from the wall. You also need to cut out any shoots that are not needed for the main framework to one bud. This method produces a more informal but still very attractive specimen.

Established pruning

Once the main framework is complete, cut back all side shoots to one bud to create flowering spurs. Chaenomeles is vigorous and will produce another long shoot in a matter of weeks, so cut these back to one bud when you see them. If the spurs become congested, remove a few of the older ones in winter. If the shrub gets unruly, it can be pruned hard back, but it is best to spread this over several years.

PRUNING CHAENOMELES

1 Cut out any crossing stems or any that form a congested area. The shoots should cover the wall or fence in an even spread.

2 Once established, cut back all side shoots to one or two buds or leaves. They grow rapidly and will need pruning several times a year.

3 Tie in all the shoots to wires stretched across the wall or fence. Failure to do this will result in the plant growing away from the wall.

ABOVE A free-standing chaenomeles, showing its sprawling natural habit, which is quite different from tightly wall-trained plants.

Roses

These are some of the most popular garden plants. Every year, there are hundreds of new varieties to add to the thousands that are already in existence. Fortunately, these all fall into distinct pruning categories so that gardeners who already grow roses have no difficulty in coping with the new arrivals. However, to anyone new to gardening, pruning roses can seem a bewildering topic. There seem to be so many varieties and different types, each requiring a different method.

In spite of the number of different types of rose and the differences in pruning each, common sense applies to them all. It is quite comforting to know how difficult it is to kill a rose by mis-pruning. It has been shown that you can simply hack off stems with a chainsaw and the rose will remain healthy and produce masses of blooms. But proper pruning is more satisfying and produces a neater result.

The key to successful rose pruning is to take your time and to wear stout gloves. Just learn about the types you have in the garden and add to your knowledge and experience as you include new roses to your collection. After a couple of attempts, you will find that rose pruning becomes second nature and your roses will bloom more beautifully each year.

LEFT Who can resist a wonderful and abundant display of roses? This is achieved through careful training and pruning, neither of which is very difficult.

Pruning roses

There are a number of different types of rose, each group being distinguished by the way it grows. The habit of growth dictates how the rose should be pruned. Fortunately, roses are very resilient plants, and it is quite difficult to kill one through mis-pruning. The worst you can do is inhibit flowering for one season.

Timing

Pruning generally takes place in three stages. The first is to cut off the flowers as they fade. The second is usually considered optional and is undertaken mainly in windy areas: in late autumn, taller shoots on bush roses can be cut back by up to half to prevent the bushes being damaged by the wind. The main pruning then takes place in late winter to early spring.

ABOVE Roses need attention throughout the year, including deadheading in summer if your display is to continue in perfect condition.

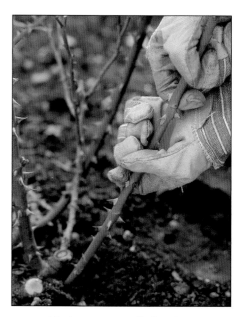

ABOVE Most roses are grafted on to a rootstock, which can produce suckers. Remove these when you see them.

Basic cuts

Cut shoots of roses back to either a bud or a shoot, preferably a strong one in both cases. Thinner wood can be cut with secateurs (pruners) while thick stems can be cut with either long-handled pruners or a pruning saw. It is important that your tools are well maintained and sharp, so that you make a clean cut with no tears or bruising. The cut should be just above a bud or shoot and should gently slope away from it so that any rain runs away and does not lie in the junction with the stem. Never cut through a stem between buds, as this will cause die-back from the point of the cut downwards to the bud. This may introduce infection into the plant or cause the stem to die back beyond the bud. This also applies to deadheading.

Training

There are several methods of training roses besides growing them as simple bushes. Long stems are usually best tied in or they will thrash about and tear other shoots

with their thorns. If allowed to grow upright, they will tend to produce flowers only at the tops of their shoots. If they are pulled down into an arc, flower buds form all along the upper surface, resulting in more prolific flowering. Tie in rose stems either with special garden ties or soft garden string. For more permanent training, use tarred string.

ABOVE A well-pruned floribunda rose showing the well-balanced shape and size of bush that should be aimed for.

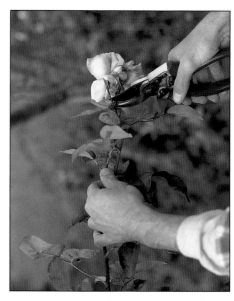

ABOVE Deadheading is important to maintain continuous flowering. Cut back to the first leaf, bud or shoot.

Deadheading

This is a routine job needed by most roses. If allowed to remain on the bush, fading flowers can look unsightly and will detract from the beauty of those that remain. At this stage, the flower's life is over and seed formation begins, which is very costly in terms of the plant's energy. By cutting off the flower heads, energy is diverted into producing more flowers. On the other hand, there are some roses that have beautiful hips, so these should not be deadheaded. As a general principle when deadheading, cut back to the first healthy bud below the faded flower. Do not just cut the flower head off at random.

Suckers

Most roses are grafted on to a rootstock, often a wild rose. From time to time this rootstock can throw up a sucker from below the graft, often from below ground. This is usually readily identifiable, as it is usually very straight and looks completely different from the main rose. It should be removed as soon as it is seen or it can take over the bush. Dig back the soil around the plant to find its point of origin. Pull it away from where it joins the rootstock. Suckers cut off at ground level will regrow.

A ROSE GARDEN There are a wide variety of roses. They all vary slightly in their initial training and established pruning, but within this variation the principles remain the same. The basic aim with all these different types of rose is to create a healthy plant, with no congestion or crossing wood that can rub against and damage other stems. The bushes and climbers should not be crowded, so that light can enter and air circulate. Deadheads should be removed to promote further flowering.

Bush roses

Bush roses are usually divided into two distinct types: hybrid teas, which produce single, large flowers, and floribundas, with clusters of flowers. These are some of the most popular of all roses, with a very wide range of colours available. Since they are relatively heavily pruned each year, they tend to take up little space. There is a certain upright formality about them, so they are mainly used in rose beds rather than in less formal, mixed beds with herbaceous plants.

Supports

Bush roses are usually grown as bushes and normally require no support at all, even when they are first planted.

Initial training

Plants are bought either as container or as bare-root plants. If you cannot plant bare-root roses straight away, heel them into a spare bit of ground, so that their roots do not dry out. Plant container roses at the same depth as they were in the pot. The best time for planting is between late autumn and early spring. Prune all

Some hybrid tea roses

'Admiral Rodney'	Christopher	'Etoile de Hollande'	Pot o' Gold
Alec's Red	Columbus	Fragrant Cloud	'Prima Ballerina'
'Apricot Silk'	Congratulations	'Grandpa Dickson'	Remember Me
'Blessings'	Dawn Chorus	'Harry Wheatcroft'	Royal William
Blue Moon	'Deep Secret'	'Lovers Meeting'	Silver Anniversary
Buxom Beauty	'Doris Tysterman'	'National Trust'	Tequila Sunrise
Cherry Brandy	Elina	Peace	Whisky Mac

the shoots back to about 10–15cm (4–6in) above the soil level to a strong, outward-facing bud. If there are any weak, damaged or badly placed (i.e. crossing or rubbing) shoots, either cut these low down to a good bud or remove them completely if necessary. If a container rose is planted at any time other than winter, leave the initial pruning until its first winter.

Established pruning

Bush roses establish very quickly and a year after planting the pruning regime will become established. Deadhead the roses once the flowers begin to fade. In windy areas, in late autumn after flowering and before the winter winds set in, reduce all the shoots by about half to prevent

wind-rock and thrashing stems. The main pruning can start at any point between mid-winter and early spring, while the bushes are still dormant. If you cut back too early, growth is stimulated and you may have to prune again after a mild winter. Start by cutting out any dead, damaged or diseased wood, as well as any thin, weak growth, then deal with what is left. In the case of hybrid teas, cut back all stems to a strong outward-facing bud about 15–25cm (6–10in) above the ground. Shorten any laterals or side shoots to two or three buds. As the plants begin to age, cut out one or two of the older stems completely at the base to encourage new growth and rejuvenate the plant. With floribundas, the pruning is very

PRUNING A HYBRID TEA ROSE

1 As with most pruning, the first task is to remove any dead, diseased or damaged wood, cutting back to a bud in sound wood.

2 Next remove some of the older wood, especially if, as here, it has die-back, caused by bad pruning in the past in which the cut was made too high above a bud.

3 Cut back the remaining growth to an outward-facing bud, 15–25cm (6–10in) above the ground, or just above the previous year's pruning.

4 Any suckers, such as the one in front of this rose, should be removed from their point of origin below ground.

PRUNING A NEWLY PLANTED BUSH ROSE Plant new bush roses between autumn and early spring. All the stems will be too long when the rose arrives from the nursery. As soon as you have planted the rose, cut all stems back to an outward-facing bud, about 10–15cm (4–6in) above the ground.

PRUNING AN ESTABLISHED HYBRID TEA Hybrid teas are a very popular type of rose for the garden, and generally these are given the severest of pruning. In spring, after removing any dead or diseased wood, cut back all the remaining shoots to within 15–25cm (6–10in) of the ground, at an outward-facing bud.

PRUNING AN ESTABLISHED FLORIBUNDA The floribundas are pruned in a similar manner to the hybrid teas, but are not treated quite so harshly. After removing all the dead, damaged or diseased wood, cut back all the remaining shoots to about 25–30cm (10–12in) above the ground and any laterals to two or three buds.

similar but need not be so drastic. After removing dead, damaged or diseased wood as well as any weak growth, shorten each stem to about 25–30cm (10–12in) from the ground. Again, any laterals can be reduced to two or three buds.

As with most roses, any suckers that appear from below the graft should be removed at their point of origin, which in many cases is below ground. If left, they will produce different growth and flowers.

PRUNING A FLORIBUNDA ROSE

1 Floribundas can get tall, so it may be necessary to cut them back by about half in the autumn in order to prevent wind-damage.

2 In the spring remove any dead, diseased or damaged wood, cutting right back to a bud or shoot in sound wood.

3 Remove any shoots or branches that are crossing others, especially if they rub against them.

Some floribunda roses

Amber Queen	Iceberg
'Anne Harkness'	Irish Eyes
'Arthur Bell'	'Korresia'
Beautiful Britain	L'Aimant
Betty Harkness	Lilli Marlene
'Bonfire Night'	'Masquerade'
Centenary	Princess of Wales
'City of Leeds'	Remembrance
'English Miss'	Sexy Rexy
Fellowship	Sunset Boulevard
'Glenfiddich'	Trumpeter

4 Cut back the remaining shoots to a basic framework, about 25–30cm (10–12in) above the ground.

5 Weak shoots such as this should be cut right back to a stronger main stem or to the main framework.

ABOVE Here, more attention is required to even out the heights of the stems to produce a more rounded bush as well as removing weaker stems and cutting back stems to a bud.

Repeat-flowering shrub roses

Shrub roses have become increasingly popular and there have been several new introductions. They tend to make larger plants than hybrid teas and floribundas and are good as specimens or in large mixed plantings. They all need minium pruning or training when they are first planted.

Modern shrub roses

Start by removing any wood that is dead, damaged or diseased. Beyond that, there is not a great deal to do other than prune back the tips of a number of the side shoots. After a few years, remove a couple of the oldest main shoots every year or two to encourage new growth and prevent congestion. Some of the modern varieties with flowers in clusters should have their shoots cut back by up to one-third.

Ground-cover roses

Most are similar to the modern shrub roses but spread sideways rather than growing upwards. Apart from taking out any dead wood, you can usually leave these to fill their allotted space. Cut them back if they

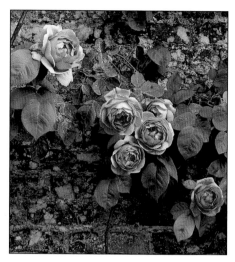

ABOVE A favourite modern shrub rose, 'Constance Spry'. This rose is not repeat-flowering but is pruned in the same way.

stray too far. After a few years, remove some of the oldest wood to rejuvenate them.

Rugosa roses

These are similar to the modern shrub roses. Remove all the dead, damaged or diseased wood and then tip-prune the longer stems. When the plants are several years old, remove one or two of the oldest stems completely to the ground to keep the shrub vigorous by promoting fresh growth from the base.

ABOVE A Bourbon rose, 'Boule de Neige', which is not pruned too severely: just reduce stems by about one-third.

Hybrid musk roses

Take out all the dead, damaged and diseased wood, then cut back all the main stems by about one-third and shorten side shoots by about half. Once the bush has matured, cut one or two of the oldest main stems to the ground each year or so to rejuvenate the plant.

Bourbons, Portlands and China roses

These are old-fashioned roses, many of some antiquity. Although

ABOVE 'Old Blush China' is, as the name implies, an old China rose. The pale pink, double flowers, produced from summer to autumn, are lightly scented.

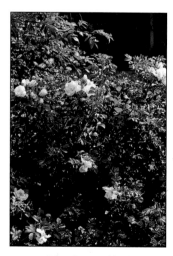

ABOVE 'Blanche Double de Coubert' is a Rugosa rose. The sweetly scented, white flowers open from pointed, pinkish buds from summer to autumn.

ABOVE 'Souvenir de la Malmaison' is a Bourbon rose with very fragrant, pale pink flowers. The flowers may be spoilt by wet weather.

ABOVE 'Madame Isaac Pereire', a Bourbon, makes a tall, loose bush and is better trained as a climber. The cerise-pink flowers are richly fragrant.

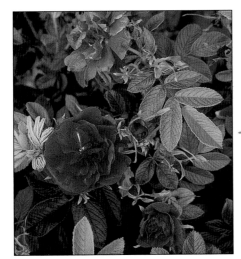

ABOVE A Rugosa rose that requires very little pruning other than removal of dead wood and tip-pruning of long stems.

PRUNING AN ESTABLISHED MODERN SHRUB ROSE Most modern shrub roses are repeat-flowering, but there are some that are single-flowering and are treated in the same way. What little pruning there is should take place in the spring. Deadheading should be carried out throughout summer. After taking out any dead, diseased or damaged wood, cut back the tips of some of the longer shoots and remove one or two of the oldest stems completely. Other than that there is little to do.

the main flush of flowers is in early summer, they are repeat-flowering. The main pruning is in late winter to early spring before growth begins. (In windy gardens, it may also be necessary to reduce very long shoots by about a quarter in autumn.) In winter, as well as cutting out any dead, damaged or diseased wood, cut all shoots back by about one-third. Once the bush has reached maturity, remove one or two of the oldest stems every year or so as a programme of continuing rejuvenation. In windier gardens, more vigorous varieties with longer shoots can be tied down to a series of arched, pliable hazel sticks which are placed just inside the perimeter of the plant. The tops of the arches should be about 1m (3ft) above ground-level. This technique keeps the shoots steady in the wind and promotes increased flowering. The whole structure should be untied when you want to prune the rose, and then rebuilt with new sticks.

Some modern shrub roses	Some ground-cover roses	Some rugosa roses	Some hybrid musk roses	Some Bourbons, Portlands and China roses
'Abraham Darby'	'Cardinal Hume'	'Agnes'	'Buff Beauty'	'Boule de Neige'
'Charity'	'Fairyland'	'Belle Poitevine'	'Callisto'	'Bourbon Queen'
'Chaucer'	'Ferdy'	'Blanche Double de	'Cornelia'	'Commandant
'Constance Spry'	'Flower Carpet'	Coubert'	'Erfurt'	Beaurepaire'
'Gertrude Jekyll'	'Ice Fairy'	'Fimbriata'	'Francesca'	'Comte de Chambord'
'Graham Thomas'	'Jacquenetta'	'F.J. Grootendorst'	'Golden Wings'	'Louise Odier'
'Jacqueline Du Pré'	'John Cabot'	'Fru Dagmar Hastrup'	'Kathleen Ferrier'	'Madame Isaac Pereire'
'Mary Rose'	'Nozomi'	'Max Graf'	'Penelope'	'Old Blush China'
'Perdita'	'Snow Carpet'	'Pink Grootendorst'	'Prosperity'	'Perle d'Or'
'Prospero'	'White Bells'	'Roseraie de l'Haÿ'	'Thisbe'	'Souvenir de la
'Warwick Castle'		'Sarah van Fleet'	'Will Scarlet'	Malmaison'
'Windrush'				

Single-flowering shrub roses

A second category of shrub roses comprises the older ones that flower only once, in the early summer. These are quintessential "English garden" plants. The soft shapes of the shrubs and subtle colours of the flowers allow them to fit in well in mixed borders, surrounded by perennials. There are a number of different groups.

Alba, Damask, Centifolia (Provence) and Moss roses

This is a large group of old-fashioned varieties, once the mainstay of many rose gardens. In spite of their single flowering, there are some gems among them. They are best pruned in summer, after they have finished flowering. First, remove any dead, damaged and diseased wood, then cut back all shoots by up to one-third of their length. After a few years, once the shrub becomes established, cut out completely one or two of the oldest main stems every year or so to promote ongoing rejuvenation. In windier gardens, tie more vigorous varieties with longer shoots down to a series of arched, pliable hazel sticks placed just inside the perimeter of the plant. The tops of the arches

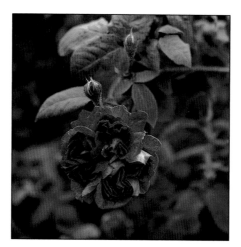

ABOVE Moss roses, such as 'William Lobb', are usually pruned in summer after flowering when shoots are cut back by about one-third.

should be about 1m (3ft) above ground-level. This procedure keeps the shoots steady in the wind and promotes increased flowering. The whole structure should be untied for pruning and then rebuilt with new sticks.

Gallica roses

The main pruning of a Gallica rose is after it has finished flowering. Take out all dead, diseased and damaged wood. Cut back the side shoots to a good shoot or to the main stem itself. As these roses tend towards dense growth, in winter remove any dead material from the

ABOVE 'Köningin von Dänemark', an Alba rose, is pruned in summer after flowering, cutting back the shoots by about one-third.

centre of the plant. It also helps to remove one or two of the oldest stems each year to help keep the shrub vigorous.

Species roses

Most species flower only once during the year. They need very little pruning beyond the removal of dead, damaged and diseased wood. You can also cut back any particularly long shoots that stray beyond their accepted bounds. Once the shrub is well established, cut out completely one or two of the oldest stems every year or so to promote replacement growth. Pruning should take place in winter.

Some Alba, Damask, Centifolia (Provence) and Moss roses

'Alba Maxima'
'Belle Amour'
'Chapeau de Napoléon'
'De Meaux'
'Fantin-Latour'
'Félicité Parmentier'
'Ispahan'
'Jeanne de Montefort'
'Königin von Dänemark'
'Madame Hardy'

'Maiden's Blush'
'Robert le Diable'
'Spong'
'Unique Blanche'
'William Lobb'

Some Gallica roses

'Alain Blanchard'
'Anaïs Ségalas'
'Belle de Crécy'
'Cardinal de Richelieu'
'Charles de Mills'
'Duc de Guiche'
'Président de Sèze'

'Tuscany Superb'
'Versicolor'

Some species roses

Rosa ekae
R. glauca
R. moyesii
R. nitida
R. pimpinellifolia
R. rubiginosa
R. sericea
R. septipoda
R. willmottiae
R. xanthina

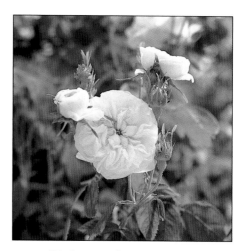

ABOVE 'Madame Hardy', one of the Damasks which are summer-pruned after flowering by cutting back the shoots by about one-third.

ABOVE *Rosa × centifolia* 'Cristata' ('Chapeau de Napoléon'), which, like all the Centifolias, is lightly pruned in summer after flowering.

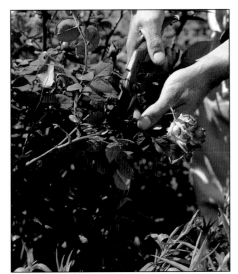

ABOVE Deadheading is vital as it ensures that the rose flowers for the maximum length of time, as well as keeping the bush neat.

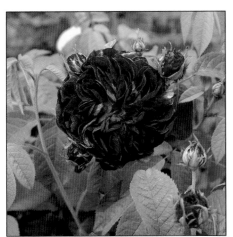

ABOVE 'Charles de Mills', one of the Gallicas. Prune in summer after flowering by cutting back the side shoots to a strong shoot.

PRUNING AN ESTABLISHED GALLICA ROSE Gallicas are pruned in summer by removing some of the side shoots back to a strong shoot or to a main stem. In winter some of the older wood is completely removed.

PRUNING AN ESTABLISHED ALBA ROSE Albas and the related roses are pruned after flowering, by cutting back most of the stems by about one-third. Some of the longer side shoots should be cut back to a main stem.

Miniature, patio and polyantha roses

Miniatures are essentially small bushes that are suitable for growing in containers or for growing anywhere where a small bush as opposed to a larger rose is required. There are three basic types: miniature roses, usually around 30cm (12in) high; patio roses, which are in effect small versions of floribunda roses; and polyantha roses, which are small bushes with clusters of small flowers.

Miniature roses

Plant the bush in the same way as a larger rose. Cut back the most sound shoots to about 8cm (3in) and discard any weak or damaged ones. During the winter of the following and subsequent years, again cut out any dead, diseased or damaged wood along with any weak shoots, or crossing or congested wood. This leaves you with next year's framework. Trim this slightly by tip-pruning all the shoots. After a few years, when the plant is well established, cut out one or two of the old stems completely so that the bush is rejuvenated. Some miniature roses respond better to harder pruning. If the above regime gives poor results, cut back the remaining shoots to about half or less of their length.

ABOVE Many gardeners are reluctant to remove weak growth, but it can congest a plant without adding to its effectiveness.

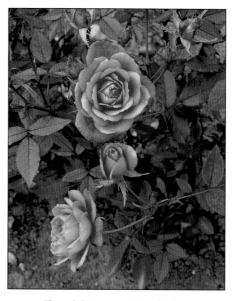

ABOVE The miniature rose Angela Rippon. Once a framework has been established, only a light tip-pruning is required.

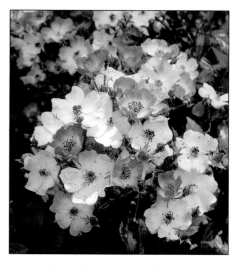

ABOVE The softly coloured 'Ballerina', which is one of those hybrid musk or polyantha roses, that can be used in either a border or a pot.

Patio and polyantha roses

A patio rose forms a compact little bush that is usually covered in wide clusters of flowers throughout the summer, until stopped by the first hard frosts of autumn. Polyantha roses are small bushes, often with a graceful habit. The airy sprays of bloom associate particularly well with herbaceous perennials and other shrubs in a mixed border.

Pruning patio and polyantha roses is relatively easy, as it is the same as for the floribundas. On planting, cut back the stems to 8–10cm (3–4in)

ABOVE A patio rose, Top Marks. Patio roses when first planted have all their stems cut back to 8–10cm (3–4in) above the ground.

ABOVE Sweet Dream, a patio rose. These are pruned in spring, cutting back all the stems by up to two-thirds to outward-facing buds.

ABOVE Sweet Magic, a patio rose, which, once established, has one or two of the oldest stems removed each year to rejuvenate it.

PRUNING AN ESTABLISHED MINIATURE ROSE Miniature roses are pruned in the spring. In spite of their miniature size, they are treated no differently from a full-size rose. Initially, prune back all the shoots to about 8cm (3in). When established, remove all dead and damaged wood along with any weak growth, and then tip-prune the remaining shoots.

PRUNING AN ESTABLISHED PATIO OR POLYANTHA ROSE Patio roses are initially pruned in the same way as miniature roses. Once established, they are generally pruned in the spring. Pruning involves removing any dead or weak wood and cutting back any remaining stems by up to two-thirds. Deadhead throughout the summer.

above ground to a strong bud. Established pruning consists of removing dead, damaged or diseased wood and cutting back all stems to about half to two-thirds of their length to an outward-facing bud or a strong shoot. Every few years, take out one or two of the oldest stems to promote new growth.

ABOVE Polyantha roses, like 'Gloria Mundi', are pruned in spring in the same way as patio roses and are best deadheaded as the flowers fade.

Some miniature roses	Some patio roses	Some polyantha roses
	Amber Hit	
Amber Sunset	Anna Ford	'Ballerina'
Angela Rippon	Bonbon Hit	'Bashful'
Apricot Sunblaze	Boys' Brigade	'Cameo'
'Baby Bio'	Bright Smile	'Coral Cluster'
Baby Masquerade	Carefree Days	Doc
Blue Peter	Conservation	'Eblouissant'
Bush Baby	Danny Boy	'Fairy Damsel'
'Easter Morning'	Festival	Fairyland
Gentle Touch	Flower Power	'Gloria Mundi'
Golden Penny	Fond Memories	'Jean Mermoz'
'Lavender Jewel'	House Beautiful	'Katharina Zeimet'
'Little Flirt'	Innocence	Lovely Fairy
Mandarin	Make a Wish	'Margo Koster'
New Penny	Our George	Marjorie Fair
Peach Sunblaze	Pearl Anniversary	'Paul Crampel'
Peek-a-boo	Rainbow Magic	'Perle d'Or'
Peter Pan	Shine On	'White Cécile Brunner'
Red Bells	Sweet Dream	'White Pet'
Robin Redbreast	Sweet Magic	
'Stars 'n' Stripes'	Thank You	
'Sweet Magic'	Top Marks	
White Cloud	Wee Cracker	

Standard roses

Standard roses have always been popular. They make excellent centre-pieces for a formal bed and also work well in containers, especially when used in pairs, perhaps placed on either side of a path, entrance or flight of steps. Standards are roses that have been grafted on the top of a tall stem, traditionally either 1.1m (40in) (full standards) or 75cm (30in) (half-standards). Within this group, there are two other categories: bush varieties, which have a hybrid tea, floribunda, miniature or patio rose grafted on to the stem, and weeping varieties, which have a spreading ground-cover or rambler grafted on to a tall rootstock.

Supports

All standards need supporting, preferably to the point just above the graft, which is the weakest point on the stem. A stout stake is needed for most, held with a proper tree or rose tie, but smaller ones in a container can be supported by a cane. If the stake rots through, breaks or weakens, replace it. Special umbrella-like frames can be purchased for training weeping varieties.

Bush standards

Most standards are purchased ready grafted and with the initial shape

ABOVE Standard roses guarding the entrance to a lawn. They are an excellent sight and are easy to prune.

already in place. However, it is possible to create your own from scratch, by grafting the desired bush on to a stem of *Rosa rugosa*, for example. As these are no more than bushes on a stalk, they are pruned in the same way as the typical plant. So, standard patio roses are pruned as for ordinary patio roses, while miniature standards are pruned as for ordinary miniatures. The only difference is that any side shoots that develop on the main stem (the rootstock) should be removed as soon as they appear.

Weeping standards

These take a bit more effort, but are still not difficult. The stems have a tendency to rise into the air rather than weep and to get a good shape it is best to tie the stems in position on an umbrella-like frame that can be purchased from most garden centres. This not only allows you to train the stems downwards but also creates an even spread of stems around the crown of the plant. Little pruning is required until the standard has fully developed. In early autumn, remove all dead, damaged or diseased wood.

Ramblers can be very vigorous, so it is a good idea to remove wood that has flowered back to one or two buds above the graft. This will prevent the standard from becoming too crowded. At the same time, reduce all side shoots to just two or three buds. On less vigorous ramblers, simply remove one or two of the oldest stems each year, so that a balance is kept and the number of stems neither increases nor decreases. Standards created from ground-cover plants are not so vigorous, but they have a tendency to become more congested, so thin out stems as necessary and tie in or cut off any shoots that persistently grow upwards.

HOW TO PRUNE A STANDARD ROSE

1 Start, as always, by removing any dead, damaged or diseased growth. At the same time, take out any weak stems.

2 Cut out any stems that cross over others, especially if they are rubbing and causing wounds. This will also reduce congestion.

3 For standard polyanthas, reduce the remaining shoots by half to two-thirds of their length. Patios should just be tip-pruned.

4 The basic framework of a standard polyantha rose. Aim for an open tulip shape that is not too crowded with stems.

PRUNING A STANDARD ROSE

Most standards already have the initial shape formed when they are purchased from the nursery or garden centre. The intention is to keep this basic framework intact without it becoming too over-crowded, especially in the centre of the bush. Weeping standards will need a slightly different treatment, especially the vigorous types.

PRUNING AN ESTABLISHED STANDARD POLYANTHA
Established pruning of standard polyanthas is to cut back all shoots by up to two-thirds after having removed dead or damaged wood and weak growth.

AN ESTABLISHED STANDARD POLYANTHA, AFTER PRUNING
The basic framework of a standard polyantha after pruning. Keep the centre open and prune to an outward-facing bud. Remove any growth on the trunk.

WEEPING STANDARDS
On vigorous weeping specimens reduce wood that has flowered to one or two buds and cut back side shoots on the remaining growth to one or two buds. Less vigorous ones should just have one or two of the oldest stems cut out. Tie in new shoots to the frame if you have used one.

ABOVE As usual, it is important to remove any dead, damaged or diseased growth from weeping standard roses.

RIGHT These weeping standard roses, with their pale pink flowers, look striking planted on either side of a pathway, leading to an entrance in the hedge.

Climbers

Many people think of climbing roses as a single group, but in fact there are two: climbers and ramblers. The distinction is more than just a whim on some ancient rose-grower's part, and it affects the way they are pruned. Climbers are to all intents and purposes the same as bush roses except that they are much taller and need some form of support. Indeed, many varieties of rose may be grown as a large bush or trained as a climber.

Supports

Climbers can be trained in a number of ways. They can be tied in to wires stretched horizontally across walls or fences, or trained up vertical structures such as posts, obelisks and tripods. They can also be trained to cover pergolas, arbours and arches. They can be allowed to scramble into trees but this is mainly the province of the ramblers. If grown in trees, they are not very easy to prune and can lose their vitality.

Some climbing roses

'Aloha'	Handel
Altissimo	'Madame Alfred
Bantry Bay	Carrière'
'Climbing	'Maigold'
Iceberg'	'New Dawn'
'Climbing Mme	'Pink Perpétué'
Caroline Testout'	'Schoolgirl'
'Danse du Feu'	Summer Wine
Dublin Bay	'White Cockade'
'Gloire de Dijon'	'Zéphirine
Golden Showers	Drouhin'

PRUNING A CLIMBING ROSE

1 A climbing rose trained around a pillar. It can be pruned *in situ* or untied, pruned and then tied back into place.

2 After cutting out dead and damaged wood and reducing flowered stems by up to two-thirds, cut out a few of the older stems.

3 After pruning tie in the remaining shoots using proprietary rose ties or soft garden string. Do not strangle the plant.

4 When the rose is in flower, remove all the faded ones by cutting out their stem back to a leaf, shoot or bud.

RENOVATING AN OLD CLIMBING ROSE

1 Sometimes it is necessary to take drastic action in order to renovate an old climbing rose. A better support also needs to be provided.

2 The thickest of the stems should be cut through with a saw. Be careful when you reach the end of the cut that the stem does not split.

3 Thinner material can be cut out using secateurs (pruners) or long-handled pruners, again taking care not to split the remaining stubs.

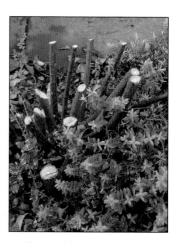

4 The resulting stool. In most cases, it would be better to spread the removal of the old wood over two or more seasons.

Initial training

No pruning is required after planting climbing roses, beyond cutting back any damaged growth. As the new stems develop, spread them out so that they cover the whole of the area and tie them in. To stimulate side shoots, lightly cut back longer shoots. Continue to tie them in as they grow.

Established pruning

Prune between late autumn and early spring. Firstly, take out completely any dead, damaged or diseased wood. Also remove any weak growth. Prune back all flowered shoots by between half and two-thirds to a strong bud or shoot. After a few years, cut out one or two of the oldest, least productive stems, either right back to the base or to a strong shoot low down. Tie in all the new growth to fill gaps and extend the framework. Avoid cutting back too vigorously, especially in the initial stages, as many climbing versions of bush varieties may revert to the bush habit.

ABOVE Deadhead as often as possible, cutting back the longer shoots that stick out over a path or into the middle of an archway.

ABOVE A mixture of climbers provides interest throughout summer. Careful pruning will ensure that no one plant dominates.

PRUNING A CLIMBING ROSE Climbing roses can be trained up a variety of supports. They tend not to be too vigorous and so are suitable for arches and the like, where more restrained growth is required. Train the rose so that it covers as much as possible of its allotted space. After flowering cut the flowered shoots up to two-thirds back to a shoot or strong bud. Also, remove any suckers that appear at the base of the rose.

Ramblers

Ramblers differ in many ways from climbers. They generally produce longer stems, which makes them suitable for scrambling through trees. Most flower best on the previous year's wood and produce a single flush. The best time to prune them is in summer after flowering.

Supports

Ramblers are very versatile. They can be trained against parallel wires on a wall or fence, or over frames such as obelisks, pergolas, arches or arbours. Many are excellent for growing up through old trees. Whatever the supports, they should be strongly mounted.

Initial training

Plant in the winter months and cut back any damaged wood. If the stems are long, prune them back to 45cm (18in) to stimulate new growth. As the new shoots appear, tie them in, spreading them out to get maximum coverage of the available space.

Established pruning

Many gardeners find the task of pruning ramblers so daunting that

ABOVE 'Bobbie James' is a very vigorous rambler that is suitable for growing through trees. Be careful when pruning because it has very vicious thorns.

Some rambling roses

'Aimée Vibert'	'Dorothy Perkins'	'Sander's White'
'Albéric Barbier'	'Félicité Perpétue'	'The Garland'
'American Pillar'	'Goldfinch'	'Veilchenblau'
'Bobbie James'	'Paul's Himalayan Musk'	'Violette'
'Debutante'	'Rambling Rector'	'Wedding Day'

they just ignore them and let them get on with it. While this approach is successful for a while, you will soon find a tangled mass of stems, with a diminution of flowering capability. When growing vigorous ramblers through tall trees, however, pruning may not be practical. In most other cases, pruning is not really difficult. Firstly, cut out any

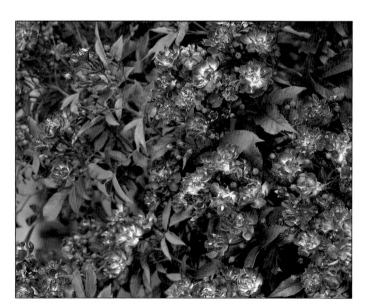

ABOVE 'Veilchenblau', unlike 'Bobbie James', is almost thornless and a good rambler for places near which people will pass.

ABOVE 'American Pillar' is a very old, small-flowered rambler that remains popular in spite of its tendency to get mildew.

PRUNING A RAMBLER

1 A sad-looking rambler that has just finished flowering. Now is the right time to prune it, starting as always by removing any dead wood.

2 Remove any stems that are rubbing against others, and any others that are causing too much congestion; an open framework is required.

3 To rejuvenate the plant, cut out some of the old stems to the base each year. Cut back other stems that have flowered to a good shoot.

4 Tie in all the shoots, spreading them widely over the support so that the whole area is evenly covered. Tie in new shoots as they develop.

dead, damaged or diseased wood. The next task is to encourage new wood. Most rambling roses produce new shoots directly from ground-level, so take out up to one-third of the oldest shoots, which will be replaced with new ones. Do this immediately after flowering, and the new growth will have matured enough to flower the following year. Some gardeners like to take the whole framework of stems off the wall and sort it out on the ground, while others prefer to attack the plant *in situ*, following each stem as it winds through the rest. If a vigorous rambler becomes overgrown from neglect, it will normally tolerate being cut back very hard to the base, but the best policy is to do a little every year.

PRUNING A RAMBLING ROSE Ramblers can become very large and cover a wide area. Some gardeners find it easier to remove the whole plant from its support and prune it on the ground, replacing the shoots when they have finished. Remove some of the old shoots from the base to encourage new flowering growth. Try to spread the shoots as widely as possible across the support.

Training over structures

Both climbers and ramblers look sensational trained over a structure of some kind, preferably over a walkway or seating area so that you are able to enjoy their beauty and scent to the full.

Choice of rose

Virtually any of the ramblers or climbers can be used. If you will be in close proximity to the rose, avoid varieties with vicious thorns, such as 'Bobbie James', and choose a thornless one, such as 'Zéphirine Drouhin'. This is less critical for larger structures where the roses are kept well away from passers-by. Another factor, especially for arbours over sitting areas, is to choose one with a good fragrance. Scented, long-flowering roses, such as 'Mme Alfred Carrière', will give much pleasure and this one has the advantage of being almost thornless. You will often find

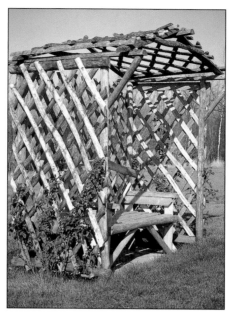

ABOVE This arbour will be much more attractive once it is covered with roses, making it a pleasant place to sit and relax.

that the roses will flower on the top of the arch or pergola, but leave the sides devoid of blooms. The best way of coping with this is to plant another, shorter-growing variety to provide flower-power for this area. For roses that flower only once, in early summer, a viticella clematis can be grown over the structure for later attraction. Clematis in this group are cut to the ground each spring, so they do not interfere with the early flowering of the rose.

Supports

Whatever the structure you create, it must be solidly constructed. A climber or rambler in full leaf, spread over a large structure, is like a large sail in a wind and will put great pressure on the construction. Check regularly that it is still in sound condition. There must be ample points at which to tie in the rose. It can be a good idea to cover the top of the structure with a wide-mesh wire netting. This is almost invisible when covered by the rose, and prevents stray stems hanging down

as well as providing plenty of tying-in points. When building an arch or any other structure, remember that the rose will project from the uprights and hang down a little way from the top, so allow extra space between posts and in the height.

Training

Plant the climber or rambler on the outside of the structure so as not to restrict the space inside. Spread the stems out so that they cover the whole width of the upright, and wrap them around if it is solid, such as a brick pier. Tie the shoots down well at the top and spread them out so that the whole area is covered. Check regularly that there are no stems, especially thorny ones, projecting outwards. Once established, prune as described on the previous pages, depending on whether the rose is a climber or a rambler.

ABOVE A rose climbing up the pillar of a pergola. Short climbers are ideal for this, with other plants providing the cover for the top.

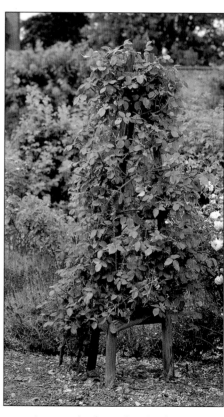

ABOVE A rose trained round a tripod. Wrapping it round a support in this manner ensures a good coverage and plenty of flowers.

Training over hoops

In smaller gardens there may not be room to accommodate large structures that can support roses. However, as long as you do not choose too vigorous a rose, it is still possible to grow many of the larger shrubs and some of the climbers and ramblers by creating a domed structure of sticks, to which the stems can be tied.

Choice of roses

Most of the larger shrub roses, as well as the climbers and ramblers, respond well if their stems are arched over. Many roses flower only at the tips of their stems, but if the stem is bent over in a low arch, it will produce flowering buds along the length of the stem. This method is suitable for shrub roses and the less vigorous climbers and ramblers.

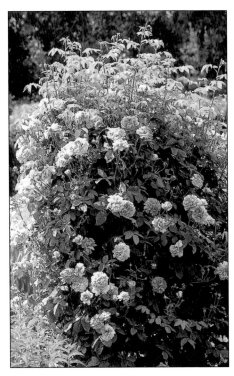

ABOVE 'Ispahan' completely covers its support, creating a dome of flowers. New shoots are beginning to appear at the top.

Supports

You can commission a blacksmith to make a set of metal hoops, but this may be expensive. An alternative is to use thin flexible sticks, such as from a hazel or pollarded sweet chestnut. Insert one end into the ground, bend it over and drive the other end into the soil. The top of the arc should be about 1m (3ft) from the ground and the ends should be about 1–1.2m (3–4ft) apart. Arrange these in a circle around the rose, with each hoop overlapping the next.

Training and pruning

Essentially the pruning is as it would be for the type of rose you are using. You should also tie in the stems of the rose in an arch around the hoops, as well as in a dome across the circle formed by the hoops.

HOW TO TRAIN A ROSE OVER A HOOP

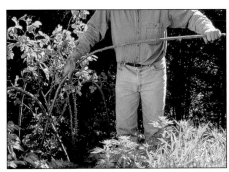

1 Choose some pliable rods – hazel is very good – that are straight and can be easily bent into a hoop without breaking.

2 Push these into the ground around the plant, forming a series of hoops to which the stems of the plant can be tied.

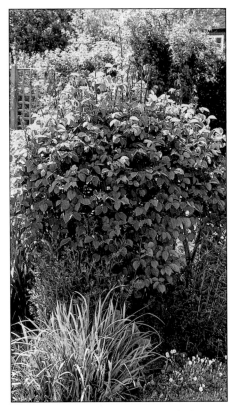

5 The rose bush in the spring, just before flowering. It is now an attractive dome of foliage and will soon be covered with a mass of flowers.

3 Carefully pull down the shoots and tie them to the hoops, arching them slightly. Some can be tied across the centre of the circle that you have created.

4 The finished plant does not look very engaging at first, but the curved stems will soon produce a mass of young flowering shoots that will look spectacular.

Training over pillars, tripods and obelisks

Sometimes it is necessary to create a vertical accent somewhere in a border, or even in the garden as a whole, but there may be insufficient room for a large structure. One of the simplest solutions is a column, either a wooden pole or a brick or stone pillar. Increasingly common are tripods and obelisks, either bought or home-made, which serve the same function.

Choice of roses

As long as they are not too vigorous, there is a wide choice of climbers and ramblers that are suitable for growing up a simple column. The ramblers are possibly best, as their stems are reasonably flexible and they respond well to training. There are a number that are relatively short, reaching only 2–3m (6–10ft), and these are the best ones from which to choose.

Supports

These should be well bedded into the ground so they will not blow over in the wind. Stems can be tied directly to the pole, but for a wider range of anchor points, wrap some wire-netting around the pole. Tripods and obelisks should have horizontal bars or wires. These prevent stems from slipping down the pole.

Training and pruning

The aim is to make certain that the stems do not run straight up the pole, otherwise you are likely just to get a few flowers at the top. Wrap the stems round in a spiral, twisting them both clockwise and anti-clockwise. This is best done when the shoots are young as they are more pliable. Once established, prune as for a climber or rambler.

TRAINING A ROSE UP A TRIPOD

1 Most tripods are in the open ground, but it is also possible to create one for smaller plants in a large container.

2 Erect a strong structure of three to five poles or canes. Make certain that they are well bedded and will not blow over.

3 Secure the canes well at the top. Use nails or wire in the case of poles and string if you are using canes.

4 Cross bars should be nailed to the uprights, or string or wire wound round to offer support for the climbing rose.

TRAINING A ROSE UP A PILLAR

1 Dig a hole at least 60cm (2ft) deep. Put in the post and check that it is upright. Backfill with earth, ramming it firmly down as it is filled.

2 Roses can be tied directly to the post, but a more natural support is created if wire netting is secured to the post.

3 Plant the rose a little way out from the pole to avoid the compacted area. Lead the stems to the wire netting and tie them in. Roses, unlike some other climbers, will need to be tied in as they climb.

4 Single-post pillars add interest to flower borders. This 'American Pillar' rose has clothed the thin post, creating a well-filled-out, irregular shape.

Training through trees

There are few more glorious sights than a large tree filled to overflowing with a rose in full bloom. To achieve this you need a suitable tree in the right place.

Choice of roses

The more vigorous ramblers, such as 'Félicité Perpétue', 'Rambling Rector' or 'Bobbie James', are ideal for this purpose. Choose one that will continue to flower well on old wood, as it is not always practical to prune a vast rambler in a tree.

Supports

Many people think an old tree is needed for this, but while the tree should be large, it must not be aged and weak. A large rose scrambling through a tree will add considerably to its weight and a weak tree will be doubly vulnerable in a gale. Choose a healthy tree such as an old apple tree that may be past its best fruiting, but is still strong.

Training and pruning

Plant the rose around 1.5m (5ft) away from the trunk of the tree (any closer and it will be deprived of light and moisture). Plant on the windy

ABOVE 'Paul's Himalayan Musk' wound round a tree. Usually the flowers appear well up into the tree, so these lower ones are a bonus.

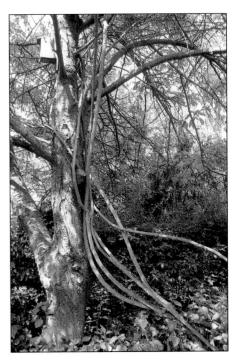

ABOVE The stems of a rambler reaching up into the top of a tree. Note how the rose has been planted away from the base of the tree.

side of the tree, which will blow the rain towards its roots and blow the stems into rather than away from the crown. Ideally, this should also be the sunny side, where there is most light. Train the stems to a rope or poles that run from the base of the rose into the lower branches of the tree where they meet the trunk. Make certain that this structure does not

chafe the tree, cushioning it if necessary. Once the rose has grown into the tree, spread out the stems and tie them in so that they clamber up through as wide an area as possible in the crown. To prune, take out any dead, damaged or diseased wood and every few years remove some of the older wood. No further pruning is usually required.

TRAINING A ROSE THROUGH A TREE

1 Plant the rose well away from the base of the tree where it can receive rain and sun. Remove any ivy in the tree or it may swamp the rose.

2 Make certain that there is plenty of well-rotted organic material dug into the soil in order to provide a good start for the rambler.

3 Plant the rose to the same depth as it was in its container or nursery bed. Spread out the roots and water well before mulching.

4 To get the rose to start to climb into the tree, tie the stems to canes that slope from the base of the rose into the tree.

Training over trellis

Trellis panels are ideal for roses. They can be seen from both sides and create a very effective screen between two areas in a garden. Trellis can also be used as breaks across a long garden or to surround a garden within a garden, or even on the garden's boundaries. You might, for example, wish to separate a kitchen garden from an ornamental garden. Lengths of trellis can incorporate an archway that is also covered with roses. Generally, trellis panels are not very high and roses grown against them are easy to train and prune.

Choice of roses

Virtually any climbing or rambling rose can be used. As long as you are prepared to control them, even the more vigorous ones can be used. Trellis is, however, ideal for shorter, less vigorous roses that stay within 2–3m (6–10ft).

Supports

Trellis can be bought as panels or can be home-made. The beauty of trellis is that it has plenty of horizontal and vertical bars to which the stems can be tied, making it easy to create an even coverage. The upright poles that support the panels must be well anchored as they will take a lot of stress, particularly in a wind.

Training and pruning

Allow plenty of space between the roses so that the overlap between adjacent plants when fully grown is minimized. Train the shoots horizontally or in a fan shape to produce as wide a coverage as possible. Tie in any loose shoots as they grow. Pruning is as for climbers or ramblers, as previously described.

TRAINING A ROSE AGAINST WALL-MOUNTED TRELLIS

1 Plant the rose at least 30cm (12in) away from the base of the wall. Ensure that the soil has been well provided with organic material.

2 After planting, remove any dead or damaged growth and cut out any weak shoots that will not develop properly.

3 Train the shoots towards the trellis with canes and tie in the stems to the trellis as soon as they reach it.

4 Spread the shoots of the rose out as widely as possible so that the rose will eventually cover as much of its allotted space as possible.

Rope swags

Roses trained on rope swags (a "calenary") can be used as a very decorative boundary or along the side of a path. A swag is a very effective way of growing climbing or rambler roses in a small garden.

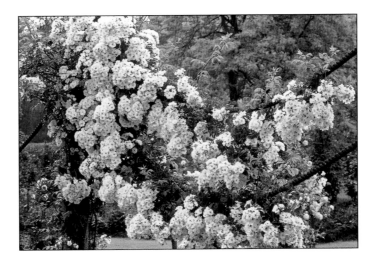

LEFT A prolific swag of roses that covers the supporting rope very well. Some gardeners prefer a narrower band of roses so that the swag-shape is more in evidence.

Choice of roses

The roses chosen should be vigorous and have flexible stems. Ramblers are the best bet. Since they will flower mainly along the ropes, it can be a good idea to plant one of the less vigorous climbers that will only climb as far as the top of the post to cover the upright with flowers.

Supports

Solid posts at distances of about 2.5m (8ft) are required to support a thick rope that will dip slightly in the middle. Do not let it dip too low as the rope will stretch with time and can sag. The rope should ideally be 5cm (2in) in diameter, the type sold by ship's chandlers.

Training and pruning

Plant the rose at the base of the upright, preferably at least 30cm (12in) away from it. Train the stems upwards in a spiral, then wrap them along the ropes. Spread the rose out to both sides of the upright. Alternatively, you might wish to plant a different rose on either side of the upright and then train the roses in different directions at the top. The pruning that is required depends on whether you use climbers or ramblers. Cut out any vigorous sideways shoots so that the line of the swag is maintained. After a few years, cut out some of the older stems in order to rejuvenate the plants. This will entail either unravelling all the stems and tying in the ones that remain or, if it is simpler, following the old stem through the swag and cutting it out in sections.

TRAINING ROSES ALONG ROPE SWAGS

Rope swags of roses are not difficult to achieve, as long as the posts are firmly embedded in the ground and the ropes are strong and well attached to their support. Choose a thick rope because thin ones can look silly. Make certain that the ropes are well secured to their poles, using galvanized or stainless-steel fittings, which will not rust.

INITIAL TRAINING Train the roses up the post, preferably winding them around to create a better coverage and then along the ropes. The stems can be wound around the ropes, but should still be tied in.

ESTABLISHED PRUNING Keep the rose pruned so that it does not become too top heavy, or the wind may destroy it. Tie in the new stems throughout the summer as well as deadheading.

Perennials and Annuals

When thinking of pruning, most gardeners will think first of woody plants, such as trees, shrubs and climbers, but, if they are to perform to their best, perennials and annuals also need some attention. The main reason why they are not included in most pruning books is that they die back each year and start afresh the following year, so they can be left to their own devices. But one of the reasons we grow them is to add to the appeal of our gardens, and they are undoubtedly improved with a bit of care.

Trees and shrubs form the backbone of our gardens, while perennials and annuals provide the filling, giving colour and excitement that changes as the months go by. Some perennials have more than one season of interest, and the garden can look quite different from one month to another. Annuals, however, flower mainly throughout the summer. The advantage with annuals is that you can change your colour scheme from one year to the next, giving quite a different feel to the garden each time.

Pruning perennials and annuals is not a difficult task, and there is not such a strict regime as with woody subjects.

LEFT A garden of softly coloured flowers. In order to maintain this level of attraction, the plants will have to be regularly deadheaded.

Pruning perennials and annuals

Perennials and annuals are the colourful mainstay of the flower garden, providing colour throughout the year in both beds and containers. While they can be left to their own devices, a little attention to pruning will extend their flowering period and enhance their attractiveness.

Perennials

Although the term "perennial" can refer to any plant that continues for more than one year, it is usually used in the garden to refer to herbaceous plants that disappear below ground at some point during the year, and reappear the following year. They are deservedly popular, both as flowering and foliage plants. On the whole, their flowering period is relatively short, but their season can be extended with appropriate pruning, and this may even result in a second flowering. Even if there is no repeat flowering, pruning will often result in a new flush of leaves, which will turn the plant into a foliage feature. The pruning of perennials is a continual process throughout the year, not, as with most shrubs, a once-a-year effort.

Annuals

What we refer to as annuals in gardening are not always annuals. Many are short-lived perennials that are better treated as annuals and thrown away at the end of the year, while others are biennials, which flower in their second year. None of this affects the pruning, except that some, such as sweet Williams (*Dianthus barbatus*) and antirrhinums, can be pruned back at the end of the year to provide another display the following year. Generally, annuals are pruned to keep them flowering for as long as possible and to ensure that they stay neat and compact over their long growing season.

ABOVE Sweet Williams (*Dianthus barbatus*) are usually grown as a biennial, but if they are cut back to new buds after flowering they will flower again the following year as a perennial.

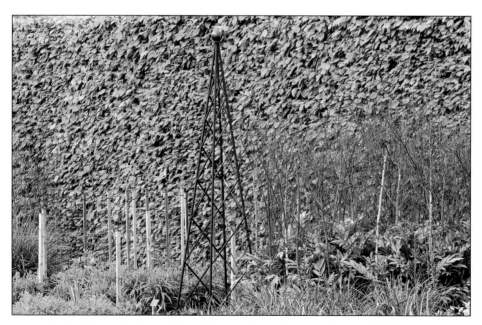

ABOVE Perennials need to be provided with some form of support. A range of different types, such as a tripod, canes and pea-sticks, can be seen in this spring picture.

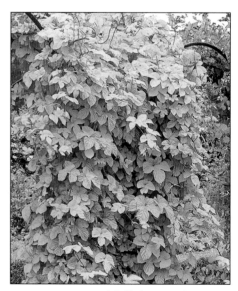

ABOVE Most perennial climbers need no pruning other than cutting down once they have finished. They are helped by having a little initial training to make certain that the shoots find their support.

ABOVE Reduce the flowering height of Michaelmas daisies (*Aster*) by cutting them down at an early stage, causing them to regrow.

ABOVE Petunias will perform over the whole summer and well into the autumn if they are regularly deadheaded to conserve energy.

ABOVE Repeatedly cutting sweet peas for flower arrangements as well as deadheading will produce a constant supply of flowers.

Tools

The tools required are likely to be those that any gardener already has to hand. The main requirement is for secateurs (pruners), although for the softer stems of annuals, scissors will do just as well. Shears are useful for quickly clipping whole plants, and some gardeners even use the lawn mower to shear over large quantities of pulmonarias, for example, in order to promote a fresh crop of leaves.

Timing

Perennials can be pruned at almost any time. In some cases, pruning starts as soon as growth emerges, when the tips of shoots are removed to promote bushiness. At the end of the season, dead stems can be cut back. In between, there is a constant removal of dead flowers and damaged stems, and adjustments of every kind. The pruning of perennials and annuals is an ongoing process, so you should wander round your borders (and containers) with secateurs in hand at least once a week, if possible. This also gives you the chance to look at and appreciate your plants.

Some gardeners like to remove the final dead stems in the autumn, while others prefer to wait until late winter so that the birds can feed on the remaining seeds.

ABOVE Hanging baskets, window boxes and other containers filled with annual flowers benefit from being deadheaded on a regular basis, as well as having any overlong stems cut back to rejuvenate and prolong the display.

Pruning and training perennials

Most gardens include some perennials in the borders, sometimes whole swathes of them creating drifts of colour. In order to maintain the appearance of such beds, as well as of the many perennials grown in containers, regular pruning is essential.

Bushing out plants

Quite a number of the more bushy perennials, such as *Dianthus*, make better plants if they are encouraged to bush out. Pinching out the growing tips stimulates side shoots to develop. This can be done with scissors or with your fingers, preferably at an early stage in the plant's development.

Dwarfing plants

In small gardens, some plants can grow too large for their allotted position. Michaelmas daisies (*Aster*), for example, may grow to 1.2m (4ft) in situations where it would be preferable to have them at 60cm (2ft). Allow the plants to develop normally. When they are about 45–60cm (18–24in) tall, you can cut them back to the ground. They will start to grow again, but should flower when they have reached only around 60cm (2ft). This works best with plants that

ABOVE Dianthus will produce more compact, bushy growth if the tips are removed from the young plants, and will flower more freely.

are clump- or mat-forming with many individual stems, such as *Aster* and *Sanguisorba*.

Deadheading

Throughout the season, deadheading will help in two ways. Firstly, flowers tend to get lost among masses of dead and dying flowers. Secondly, seed formation uses up a lot of the plant's energy, and if the flower-heads are removed before this gets under way, all this energy is diverted into providing more flowers. The flowered stems of some perennials should be cut right to the base

(single-flowered stems), while others should be cut back to the first bud or shoot, which will then branch out and produce further flowers.

Cutting back for foliage

Some plants, such as many of the geraniums, *Alchemilla* and *Pulmonaria*, will produce a second flush of leaves if the plant is cut back completely after flowering. In most cases, the foliage will be vigorous enough to turn the plant into an effective foliage plant. If the old leaves are left on, they can look lacklustre and be a host to mildew and other fungal diseases.

MAKING A CAT'S CRADLE

1 Push some canes into the ground in a random pattern around and through the plant. Cut off the tops of the canes so that they will be hidden when the plant grows.

2 Tie strings around the canes, forming an interlaced pattern of individual cells through which the plant stems will grow.

3 The finished support. The network of strings will prevent the stems, once they have grown, from falling over, and yet it will remain hidden.

DIFFERENT METHODS OF SUPPORT

1 A proprietary plant support. The uprights are pushed into the ground and then the stems grow through the mesh, providing a strong support.

2 Proprietary interlinked stakes can be used to support plants by placing them around and, if necessary, through the middle of the plant.

3 For larger areas or drifts of plants sheep netting or other large-mesh netting can be supported between strong stakes.

Autumn clear-up

As the year progresses, more and more plants will have finished flowering and the borders will gradually fill up with dead or dying stems, leaves and flowers. If the borders still have plenty of late-flowering plants, the old material should be removed to show up the remaining ones to their best advantage. Once the majority have finished, there are two differing opinions as to what should be done. Some gardeners leave the remaining stems over winter so that birds can gather seed and insects during the winter months. Then everything is cut down in spring. Others like to cut down everything as soon as

4 For more upright plants such as delphiniums, a cylinder of large-mesh wire-netting can be used. Support this with a strong stake.

possible to keep the garden neat and save time the following spring. If you do leave them till spring, be certain to cut the dead material away before the new shoots appear at the base, as it can be difficult to cut this

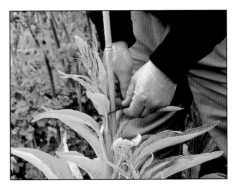

5 For single-stemmed plants a cane can be inserted behind the plant, where it is less likely to be seen, and the stem fastened with string or ties.

out without damaging the new growth. Often a compromise is the best solution, cutting back some plants to reduce the workload later, but leaving enough for the birds to enjoy in the autumn.

USING PEA STICKS

1 If available, a cheap method of support is to use hazel branches pushed into the ground around the growing plant.

2 The tips of the branches are bent over and intertwined – and tied if necessary – to form a network of twigs through which the plant stems grow.

3 Support climbers and taller clumps of plants with bunches of sticks, pushed firmly in the ground and tied together.

4 When cutting back plants, do not leave it too late or the spring growth will make it difficult to remove the old stems without damaging the new ones.

Pruning annuals

Annuals are regaining some of their former popularity, not so much as bedding plants in beds and borders, but as interesting subjects for containers. To make sure they perform at their best, they need constant pruning. Just checking them over once a week will improve them considerably.

Shaping the plants

Many annuals benefit from being pinched out to make them more bushy. Taking out the tips of the main shoots as soon as the plant starts to develop, either with scissors or with your fingers, will make the plant produce more shoots. Constant pinching out will produce a very dense, bushy plant, and this technique can also be used to shape plants. For example, by pinching out side shoots at a certain distance from the main stem, you can make some plants grow taller to form dense columns or pyramids. Others, cascade chrysanthemums being a good example, can be shaped to form dense cascades of flowers. The upright shoots of many trailing plants that are used in hanging baskets and other containers can be removed to encourage the plant to trail.

ABOVE Straggly plants can be cut back toward late summer so that they are more compact and neater with new foliage and flowers.

TIDYING UP

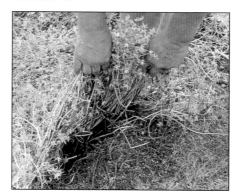

1 Once annuals have started to produce seed they should either be removed or cut back to prevent too much self-sowing.

2 The trimmings or the removed plants can be put on the compost heap, the heat from which should kill any remaining seed.

DEADHEADING ANNUALS

1 Dead flowers running to seed in an annual display not only spoil its appearance but also slow down the production of new flowers.

2 Cut off the dead flowers with secateurs (pruners) or scissors if it is easier. Some flowers can just be pulled off by hand.

3 The same window box after the dead flowers have been removed. It looks more attractive and will produce more flowers.

PINCHING OUT

1 Many annuals have a tendency to grow tall and straggly, but these can be improved by pinching out the tops to make them bush out.

2 (*right*) This *Senecio cineraria* has bushed out into an attractively shaped plant after the tip of the central shoot was removed.

Annual climbers

A number of the annual climbers, sweet peas (*Lathyrus odoratus*) being a good example, benefit from the removal of the tips of the main shoots. This encourages the plant to produce plenty of side shoots, which can be spread widely to cover a large area. Allowing the leading shoot to develop by itself will often result in a tall, spindly plant that does not flower freely.

ABOVE *Thunbergia alata*, a short-lived perennial grown as an annual, is a superb climber that will quickly hide its support.

Deadheading

As soon as the flower of an annual is pollinated, it will start setting seed. This is very expensive in terms of the plant's energy. If the flower is removed before the seed develops, all this energy is channelled into new flowers as the plant continues to try to reproduce itself. Far more flowers, and a longer flowering season, will be achieved by deadheading. Besides, the plant will look much more attractive without the dead flowers.

Rejuvenating

As the season progresses, so the stems of annuals grow longer and longer. They can look particularly straggly in containers. In most instances, these can be cut back not only to make the plant look neater, but also to rejuvenate it so that it produces new stems. These new stems will often produce larger flowers than the ones produced at the tips of straggling stems. The superb baskets you see in the autumn are not just the result of good feeding and watering, but also constant pruning.

In some cases, flowers may take a while to reappear, but usually the new foliage that is produced will add a fresh note to the display. Foliage, in many cases, is just as important as flowers in an arrangement.

CUTTING SWEET PEAS

1 Most annuals will produce a lot more flowers if the developing seed pods are cut off, as setting seed uses a great deal of energy.

2 Cutting flowers for indoor decoration will help to encourage the formation of even more flowers. They run to seed if left uncut.

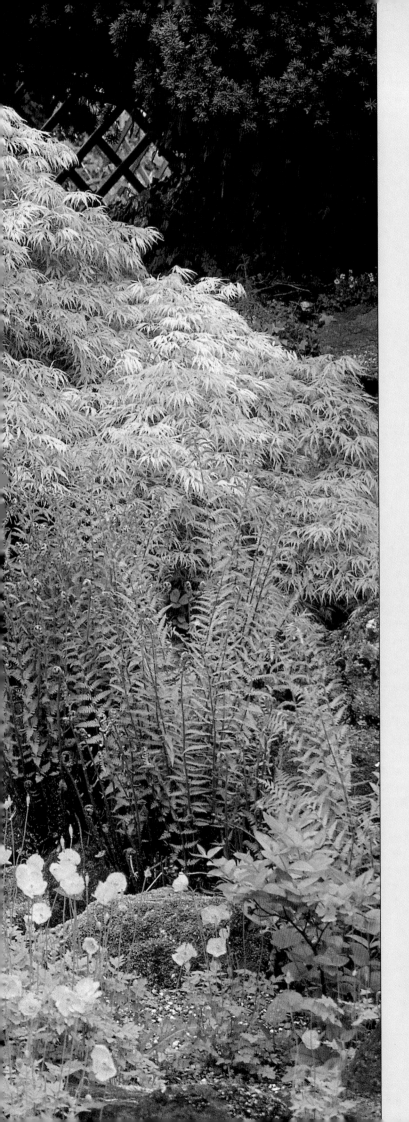

Directory of Ornamental Plants

The preceding pages give detailed information on strategies for pruning most ornamental trees, shrubs and climbers. The following is an alphabetical directory of plants, giving times and methods of pruning each plant. The plants listed are those that are among the most commonly grown in gardens.

Some pruning techniques are more involved than others, but none is beyond the capabilities of most gardeners. Pruning, like anything else, takes practice, but you will soon be able to prune the range of plants growing in your garden with confidence. If you are in any doubt, simply err on the safe side and do not take off too much. It is mainly when pruning evergreens (including many conifers) where caution has to be exercised, as some are not quite so willing to reshoot from old wood. Generally, trimming back into the current year's growth is safe.

In all cases, remove dead, damaged or diseased wood as well as any weak wood as a matter of routine. Also follow the general principles of pruning. For example, when cutting back, do so to a strong bud or to a strong shoot. If you follow these simple rules, then the plants in your garden will perform well year after year.

LEFT Maples generally need no pruning unless they outgrow their space. If you need to cut them back, do so in winter and be careful not to spoil their natural shape.

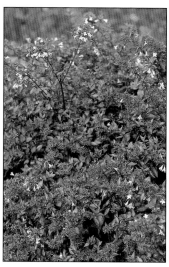

Abelia × grandiflora

ABELIA
Abelia
An evergreen shrub that flowers in summer on the previous year's wood. The main pruning is in the summer after flowering when some of the oldest wood is removed to encourage new growth from the base, which generally breaks readily. A second pruning is required in early spring to remove any dead wood and any stems that have been damaged during the winter. Some of the more tender varieties are grown as wall shrubs and new shoots should be tied into wires as they appear.

ABUTILON
Flowering maple
Tender evergreen and deciduous shrubs that are mainly grown in pots and put out in summer or given a warm, sheltered place in cooler areas. Wall-trained specimens (*A. vitifolium*) should be allowed to develop with a leader, a replacement being encouraged if the original one is broken. The main pruning is deadheading (important on this plant).

Abutilon megapotamicum

No other pruning is usually required. *A. megapotamicum* can also be wall-trained as well as planted as a free-standing shrub. Older wood can be cut out in mid-spring and the previous year's wood cut back by about one-third. Any wood that has died should be cut back to a good shoot.

ACER
Maples
Deciduous trees that can be grown with clear trunks (especially those with attractive bark) or as multi-stemmed trees. Pruning should only be carried out when the trees are dormant, in winter, otherwise they bleed badly. Large varieties can be trained as central leader trees and little subsequent pruning is required. Multi-stemmed species and varieties should be pruned as a bush tree on a short leg or trunk. Once developed, little further pruning is necessary. Some variegated varieties revert and any such shoots should be removed when they are seen, even in summer (if caught at this stage the cuts are too small for bleeding to be a problem).

ACTINIDIA
Actinidia
Twining, mainly deciduous climbers that are grown for their foliage. Best suited to training on walls or fences. Pruning should take place in the latter half of winter or early spring. On planting, cut back stems to a few strong buds on each. Train five or six of the strongest resulting shoots on to the support, spreading them widely. Remove the rest of the shoots. In the next winter, cut back all shoots by half to two-thirds and tie in the new shoots during the summer. From now prune only to contain its

Acer palmatum

Actinidia kolomikta

size, cutting back shoots to the desired length. Remove some of the old wood in late winter to promote new growth.

AKEBIA
Chocolate vine
A vigorous deciduous climber that twines for support. It can be grown on any support used for climbers. Allow five or six shoots to develop and tie these in, spreading them out. Cut back by about two-thirds to promote new shoots and tie these in as necessary, as they develop. Once established, the plant can become very vigorous and need cutting back to contain it. Remove some of the old shoots from time to time. It is an early flowerer, and any pruning should take place after this, in mid- to late spring.

ALNUS
Alder
Deciduous trees. They can be grown as either single- or multi-stemmed trees. Initial training is needed if a single stem is required but the plant will usually develop into a multi-stemmed tree of its own accord. No pruning is required once fully grown although many, if they grow too large, can be pollarded, and will readily regenerate from the stump. Any pruning that is required can be done in winter.

AMELANCHIER
Deciduous trees or large shrubs. With care these can be grown as a single-stemmed tree, but they are more inclined to grow with multiple stems. The best time to tackle any pruning is during the winter. During initial training and subsequent pruning, the main aim should be to ensure that the branches stay open and do not

Amelanchier lamarckii

become crossed and congested. *A. stolonifera* produces suckers around the base and these need to be controlled to prevent it becoming vastly overgrown.

AMPELOPSIS
Vigorous, deciduous climbers, grown mainly for their foliage, that cling with the aid of tendrils. They will grow on most types of support, including trees. Little initial training is required other than tying in to its support. In positions where it can ramp about, it can be left to its own devices, but elsewhere, especially on walls, it should be controlled by pruning back long shoots in spring if necessary to near the main branches. In summer, cut back any excessive growth to a strong bud. Make certain that it does not find its way into gutters and under the eaves.

ARBUTUS
Strawberry tree
Evergreen trees with interesting bark. They are generally open, shrubby trees. They need good staking until they are established. Little initial training is required unless you want to train them as a standard tree, in which case the early removal of the lower branches is necessary. Thereafter little pruning is required beyond the removal of damaged wood. Any pruning should take place in late spring.

AUCUBA
Aucuba
Large evergreen shrubs that are used either as free-standing shrubs or as hedging. After planting, cut back the shoots by roughly one-third to make them bush out. Repeat the following spring. Once established, cut

back any overlong stems, reaching well into the bush. Otherwise, no pruning is required. If it outgrows its space or becomes bare at the base, cut hard back and it will reshoot. If used as a hedge, trim with secateurs (pruners), as shears or hedge cutters will cut the large leaves in half, spoiling the appearance.

AZARA
Azara

Evergreen shrubs that are marginally tender. They can be grown in the open in warmer areas, but elsewhere are best trained as fans against a wall. They are usually grown as multi-stemmed shrubs and need minimal training or pruning. They can be grown as hedging and will take well to clipping, but this usually means that the fragrant spring flowers are lost. They can be cut hard back if necessary. Prune in spring, after flowering.

BERBERIS
Barberry

A very popular genus of evergreen and deciduous shrubs with small leaves, clusters of yellow or orange flowers and colourful berries. Many have very spiny stems, so it is advisable to wear gloves when pruning. They can be grown as multi-stemmed shrubs or used in a formal or informal hedge and will need little or no formative training. They can easily be kept to size as they take pruning well, but it is better to choose carefully from the many varieties so that the plant can be allowed to develop its natural shape. There is usually no need to prune except to keep the plant in bounds, or to take out some of

the older wood to rejuvenate it, although this seems to be rarely necessary. Larger specimens can become bare at the base. In this case cut back the longer stems to a suitable new shoot to re-clothe the lower part of the shrub. Generally, pruning is done in the winter.

PRUNING BERBERIS

1 Berberis can become overgrown, with the flowers and leaves well above head height, while the base is just a mass of bare stems.

2 As always, the first task should be the removal of any dead, damaged or diseased wood. This will then give you a clear idea of what is left.

3 Take out some of the wood that is causing congestion. A number of these stems can be thinned out to the plant's advantage.

4 While thinning, look out for any shoots that cross and rub against other branches. These should ideally be removed.

5 Continue through the plant, leaving young material to develop but cutting out older wood, so that the plant is rejuvenated.

6 Finally, shape the outside of the shrub. Always prune back to a strong shoot or to a healthy-looking bud.

BETULA
Birch

Deciduous trees, generally with attractive bark. There are several weeping forms. Little training and pruning are required, although it is desirable that they are kept as a central-leader tree and any pruning should be done with this in mind. Generally they are pruned with a bare trunk, but one or two species are more shrublike and will produce more than one leader, or branch from ground level to develop as multi-stemmed bushes. Weeping forms sometimes develop a drooping trunk. Tie this firmly to a strong stake to keep it upright until the wood has developed sufficiently for it to stand upright. Remove any shoots that appear below the graft of a weeping variety, as these

will tend to grow upright and will be out of character with the rest of the tree. Birches tend to weep sap when cut, so the best time to prune is autumn or early winter.

Berberis aristata

Berberis 'Georgeii'

Betula pendula

BOUGAINVILLEA

Vigorous deciduous or evergreen climbers with insignificant flowers that are surrounded by very brightly coloured bracts. They are tender plants and must be grown in warm positions, which means they are most frequently grown against the walls of buildings. In cooler climates they must be grown in containers and overwintered inside. Strong trellis or wire supports are required to get an even spread. Initial training is important. Tie in five or six of the strongest shoots, removing the rest. Spread them out so that they cover the widest possible area. Cut these shoots back to about 15cm (6in) to a strong shoot and then treat as a fan until the whole of the space is covered. To prevent overcrowding, any congested shoots should be removed in spring. Also in spring, cut back all side shoots to two or three buds to form a spur system, as with *Chaenomeles*. After flowering, cut all the flowered stems back to a non-flowering shoot. If they become overgrown, they can be cut back hard, though it is best to do this selectively, taking out a few older shoots each year.

BRACHYGLOTTIS
Brachyglottis

In the garden, these are mainly evergreen shrubs, although the genus also includes trees and perennials. It is still often referred to by its previous name, *Senecio*. Little initial training is required and pruning is restricted mainly to keeping the rather straggly shrub in shape. The foliage is mainly silver and the flowers yellow. Regular hard pruning in spring will improve the quality of the foliage but will prevent flowering (in any case, many gardeners grow it just for the foliage and cut off the flowers before they open). If flowers are required, prune after flowering to ensure flowers the following year. Overgrown shrubs can be cut back hard, but it is better to take out a few of the older stems each year. Old shrubs are best replaced.

Buddleja davidii 'Dartmoor'

BRUGMANSIA
Angels' trumpets

A small genus of tender evergreen shrubs and trees, grown for their large flowers and still often referred to as *Datura*. In cool climates, they are best grown in containers and overwintered inside. Wear gloves when pruning as some parts contain toxic substances. Prune hard in spring before growth starts, cutting back to strong buds close to the ground or to one or two buds on low side shoots. Gradually extend the framework. If the plant gets too large, cut it back hard. Deadhead after flowering.

BUDDLEJA
Butterfly bush

Deciduous shrubs grown for their flowers and foliage. There are basically three types of buddleja from the point of view of pruning. Only one group is cut back hard, but all will take hard pruning, so if you make a mistake there is no lasting damage (though flowers for that season are

Callistemon citrinus

likely to be lost). *B. davidii* and its cultivars are pruned back hard to within 30cm (12in) of the ground, early each spring. *B. crispa* and *B. fallowiana* are pruned in the same way. *B. alternifolia* flowers on the previous year's wood and can be pruned after flowering. Cut back the old flowered shoots to a non-flowering shoot or strong bud. Occasionally take out some of the oldest wood completely. *B. globosa* flowers on new wood produced from the previous season's growth. It requires very little pruning. Take out a little old wood in spring to rejuvenate the plant. If the plant becomes too large with age, it can be pruned back hard to renovate it.

BUXUS
Box

Evergreen shrubs grown mainly for hedging and topiary. As a free-standing shrub, little

Camellia 'Cornish Spring'

formative or subsequent pruning is required. For hedging or topiary, cut the young plant back hard to promote bushy growth, then trim to shape as it grows. Once developed, trim as often as necessary to keep its shape. Box can be cut back hard if necessary, but be warned: the old wood is very hard.

CALLISTEMON
Bottlebrush

Tender evergreen shrubs. In cooler areas, grow in containers and move inside for winter or plant against a warm wall. Generally, no pruning is required, although stopping the plant, by removing the tips of the new shoots, can be done initially to produce bushy growth. Wall specimens can be tied in to wires or trellis.

CAMELLIA
Camellia

Evergreen shrubs and trees. Little pruning is needed apart from removing any damaged wood or any shoots that produce flowers

PRUNING BUDDLEJA

1 Buddlejas put on a lot of growth during the year and most will need to be pruned back drastically in the spring.

2 Cut back all the stems to one or two buds of the previous year's wood. This should be just above ground-level.

3 The finished stool. Remove one or two of the oldest stems right back to the base, in order to stimulate new growth.

that are not typical of that variety. A bushy shape can be encouraged on young plants by carefully pruning young shoots back in spring. Overgrown plants can be cut back hard in spring.

CAMPSIS
Trumpet vine
Deciduous climbers grown for their foliage and flowers. They are best grown against tall walls using wires as supports. When planted, cut back shoots to about 15–20cm (6–8in) from the ground to promote strong growth, which should be trained as widely over the space as possible. It flowers on new growth, so cut back new shoots in the spring to one or two buds of the main stem. To renovate, the whole plant can be cut back to within 30cm (12in) of the ground, but it is better to remove a few of the oldest stems each year and tie in replacements.

CARPINUS
Hornbeam
Deciduous trees, grown mainly as hedging, but also as trees. For trees, train as a feathered or central-leader tree. Thereafter, little pruning is required. For hedging, trim as required, usually once or twice a year.

CARYOPTERIS
Caryopteris
Deciduous shrubs grown for their foliage and flowers. Initial training consists of pruning each stem back to just a few buds to create a good framework. Established

Ceanothus griseus

pruning consists of cutting back the previous year's growth in spring to within a bud or two of the old wood. Do not cut back into old wood as this is reluctant to produce new growth.

CASTANEA
Sweet chestnut
These are mainly grown to produce fruit or wood and are suitable only as specimen trees in big gardens, where they should be trained as central-leader trees. Little pruning is required once established.

CATALPA
Bean tree
Deciduous trees. Initially train as a leader tree with a bare trunk, after which it will naturally branch out to create a large, open-crown tree. Once established little pruning is needed. Once trees become old, they may become unsafe. Branches can be cut back, and will rejuvenate. By this stage, however, professional help may be advisable. Catalpas can also be coppiced or pollarded and, if so, will produce larger leaves.

CEANOTHUS
California lilac
Deciduous or evergreen shrubs. Evergreens are dealt with in *Ornamental shrubs*. Deciduous varieties are more frequently grown as free-standing specimens than the evergreens. Initial training should aim to produce a strong framework. Cut back all stems by half to two-thirds to an outward-facing bud. The following year, in spring, cut back the previous year's growth, again by half to two-thirds. Once established, cut back all flowered stems by about half and other shoots to just one or two buds. Cut out completely any congested or unproductive wood. As with evergreen ceanothus, deciduous varieties do not break easily from old wood, so do not cut back into it. Renovation is seldom successful.

CERATOSTIGMA
Ceratostigma
Mainly evergreen and deciduous shrubs. In most colder climates they are cut back each winter by frost. In spring, cut all stems back to about 5cm (2in) above the ground. In milder areas, where the stems are retained, build up a framework and then cut back the previous year's growth each spring to within a bud or two of the old wood.

CERCIDIPHYLLUM
Katsura tree
A deciduous tree. This normally grows naturally as a multi-

Cestrum parqui

stemmed tree, despite its upright growth. Generally, no initial or subsequent training is required. Allow the tree to develop to its natural shape.

CERCIS
Judas tree
Deciduous trees and shrubs. *C. japonicum*, the Judas tree, is grown mainly for its early flowers. It normally forms a multi-stemmed tree which should be allowed to develop naturally. Cut out any damaged and dead wood, as it can be affected by coral spot.

CESTRUM
Deciduous or evergreen shrubs. *C. parqui* is possibly the hardiest and the one most commonly grown in cooler areas. No initial training is required. If cut to the ground by severe frosts, cut back the dead material at the base. Even in a mild winter, the tips die back after flowering and should be cut back to a bud in sound wood. Remove some of the older wood each year. It tends to sucker, so it may also be necessary to remove some of the new suckers to contain its growth. Prune in early spring.

CHAENOMELES
Flowering quince
Deciduous or evergreen shrubs. They are usually trained as wall shrubs but they can also be grown as free-standing garden shrubs. These can become large and straggly, so are really suitable only for large gardens. They need little pruning beyond cutting back the longer stems if they outgrow their allotted space. Take out one or two of the oldest stems each year to rejuvenate the plant.

PRUNING CERATOSTIGMA

1 Ceratostigmas put on a lot of growth each year, and become rather bushy. In colder climates, it is usual to cut back all of this growth.

2 There is no need to cut the shrub stem by stem: just take a pair of shears and cut it to 5cm (2in) above the ground.

3 The stubby remains will all grow back. In warmer areas, cut back the previous year's growth to one or two buds of the old wood.

Cistus × cyprius

CHOISYA
Mexican orange blossom

Evergreen shrubs. Little if any initial pruning is required as they naturally form a fine bush. Established pruning consists mainly of cutting back flowered stems to keep the bush compact and to promote further flowering. They are hardy, but frost can cut back some shoots. Remove these in spring. If necessary renovate by cutting back hard in spring.

CISTUS
Rock rose

Evergreen shrubs. Little initial pruning is required although some may need tip-pruning to encourage them to bush out. Once established, little pruning is needed beyond the removal of any dead wood. Plants can become straggly, but they resent being cut hard back as they will not break from old wood.

CLEMATIS
Clematis

Evergreen and deciduous climbers grown for their flowers. Pruning is dealt with in a separate section.

PRUNING CISTUS

1 Cistus form dense, compact evergreen shrubs. They need very little pruning, either at the initial or established stages.

2 Take out any dead wood and trim back lightly to the previous year's growth if you need to keep the plant within its space.

CLERODENDRUM
Clerodendrum

Mainly deciduous or evergreen shrubs. Of the two commonly grown in gardens, *C. bungei* is a suckering shrub that is usually cut back by winter frosts in cool areas. In spring, cut out all frosted stems to the ground. Remove any suckers as necessary to restrict the plant's spread. *C. trichotomum* is more shrubby and should be trained on a short leg. Once formed, cut back the previous year's growth to one or two buds in spring. Any suckers that arise should be taken off below ground-level at source.

CLIANTHUS
Parrot's bill

Evergreen shrubs. They are best grown against a wall, tied in to wires or trellis. Initial pruning consists of cutting back the stems on planting to produce strong shoots, which should be trained in to the wall. In spring stop these shoots to produce more, until the

wall is covered. Once covered, pruning is restricted to removing a few of the oldest stems each year in spring back to a new shoot, and tying in the new growth to fill the gaps as it appears.

COBAEA
Cup-and-saucer vine

Evergreen and herbaceous climbers of which only one, *C. scandens*, is in general cultivation. This is a perennial but is often treated as an annual and discarded each autumn. Initial training consists of stopping the shoots to make it bush out and tying it into supports, aiming for as wide a spread as possible, for maximum interest. Where grown as a perennial, it should be cut back in spring, reducing the previous year's growth by half to three-quarters.

COLUTEA
Bladder senna

Deciduous shrubs. The simplest pruning method is to let the

shrub develop naturally and restrict pruning to cutting out just a few of the oldest stems each spring. However, for a tighter shrub and a longer flowering period, it can be cut back hard almost to ground-level each spring. Shrubs that have not been pruned can be renovated by cutting them hard back in spring.

CORNUS
Dogwood

Deciduous trees and shrubs. Trees should be allowed to develop naturally as single-leader trees. If left to their own devices, however, many (*Cornus mas*, for example) develop as multi-stemmed trees or large shrubs. Once established, very little pruning is required. Removal of dead or damaged wood and any wayward branches should be carried out in winter. Shrubs vary, but those grown for their winter stems, mainly cultivars of *C. alba*, need to be cut back to just above soil level in early spring. If grown for their flowers, little pruning is required beyond taking out a few of the oldest stems each spring to rejuvenate the plant. Overgrown shrubs can be renovated by cutting back hard, almost to the ground.

CORYLOPSIS
Winter hazel

Deciduous shrubs grown for their winter catkins. Let the new plants develop naturally and prune only to remove dead wood. If it is necessary to cut back longer branches that have outgrown their space, do so after flowering (or

Clematis

Clematis 'Lasurstern'

Cornus alba sibirica

Cotoneaster conspicuus

Crataegus laevigata

Cytisus battandieri needs little pruning except for the removal in spring of any wayward or crossing shoots that may rub against others.

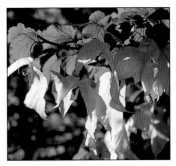

Davidia involucrata

cut them during flowering and use them in flower arrangements).

CORYLUS
Hazel
Deciduous trees and shrubs grown for their flowers, foliage and fruit. Those grown for flowers and foliage are usually grown as multi-stemmed plants. No initial training is required and little subsequent pruning, except to remove a few of the oldest stems each year once the shrub is established, to rejuvenate the plant. Overgrown shrubs can be cut back hard for renovation.

COTINUS
Smoke bush
Deciduous trees or shrubs. Little initial training is required, but subsequent pruning depends on what you want from the plant. Large, well-coloured leaves are best achieved by pruning hard back to one or two buds on a framework of branches 60cm (2ft) or so from the ground. Larger shrubs will have good, but not so spectacular, foliage plus the wonderful flower heads which

develop on older wood. To achieve this, restrict pruning to the removal of dead wood and any overlong or wayward stems. Renovation can be achieved by cutting back hard in early spring.

COTONEASTER
Cotoneaster
Evergreen and deciduous shrubs, grown for their foliage, flowers and fruit. The main garden species, *C. horizontalis*, can be grown either as a low-growing shrub or as a wall shrub. For the prostrate form no initial training is required and pruning should be kept to a minimum, as it is reluctant to break from old wood. To grow against a wall, provide support initially. Plants will soon grow flat against the wall. Remove any badly placed stems. Other species require minimal pruning.

CRATAEGUS
Hawthorn
Deciduous trees and shrubs. Some are grown as trees in gardens, but it is mainly used as country-style hedging, and is often known as quickthorn.

Flowering forms are usually trained as single-stemmed trees with a clear trunk, but if the leader is damaged they can become multi-stemmed. No pruning is generally required. If they become overgrown, they can be renovated by cutting back almost to ground-level. For hawthorn hedges, see *Hedges*.

CYTISUS
Broom
Semi-deciduous shrubs. Little pruning is required for the majority, but the most commonly seen broom, *C. scoparius* and its many cultivars, can become rather straggly. To prevent this, cut back the previous year's growth by about half to two-thirds after flowering. Do not cut back into old wood, as it does not break easily.

DAPHNE
Daphne
Evergreen or deciduous shrubs. These need little or no initial training or subsequent pruning – in fact, pruning is best avoided as it can promote die-back. Cut out any dead growth as soon as it is seen.

DAVIDIA
Handkerchief tree
A large deciduous tree grown for its decorative bracts, which look like handkerchiefs and surround the inconspicuous flowers. Initial training should be confined to ensuring that it develops as a single-leader tree. Keep the trunk clear of side shoots below the bottom branches.

DEUTZIA
Deciduous shrubs grown for their flowers. They produce a lot of basal growth which can grow tall and ungainly, so shorten stems initially to promote bushiness. Once established, cut back flowered shoots to a new shoot and cut out a few of the oldest stems each year to promote new growth from the base.

1 Heathers can get very straggly and it can then be difficult to get them back to a compact shape without replanting.

2 Lightly trim over the plant, removing the flowered wood back to one or two buds. This can be done with a pair of shears.

3 The finished plants. Do not cut back too hard as they will not recover if they are pruned back into the old wood.

Deutzia × elegantissima

Euonymus europaeus

ECCREMOCARPUS
Chilean glory flower
An evergreen climber. It is perennial but is often treated as an annual. In warmer areas, it will overwinter. In cooler ones, it can be cut to the ground by frosts, but will usually regenerate from the base. It can be trained up a trellis or up wires. It has tendrils and is self-clinging, but may need encouragement. On a young plant, pinch out the tips of the shoots so that it bushes out and provides a good coverage. Each spring, cut the previous year's growth almost back to old wood, to a strong bud.

ELAEAGNUS
Elaeagnus
Evergreen and deciduous shrubs and trees. These naturally form bushy shrubs and no initial training is required. Similarly, little established pruning is required, other than cutting back longer stems to maintain control, if necessary. This can be done in late summer. They will all take clipping well and although this may spoil the natural shape of the plant, it can be used to good effect in hedging. *E. × ebbingei*, in particular, makes a good hedge. For renovation they can all be cut back hard.

EMBOTHRIUM
Chilean fire bush
Evergreen trees. They can be trained as a single-leader or multi-stemmed tree. For the latter, no special initial training is required, but to create a single-stemmed tree, initial training and pruning should be directed towards creating a clear trunk up to 1.2–2m (4–6ft) high. Little established pruning is required. Both types are likely to sucker,

and unless they are needed as replacement growths, suckers should be removed at source.

ERICA
Heather
Evergreen shrubs and trees. The majority of heathers grown in gardens are the low-growing shrubs. These require no initial training, but it is important to clip them over once a year, after flowering, to stop them becoming straggly. They do not regenerate from old wood, so just shorten the previous season's growth to one or two buds. It is difficult to renovate old plants. Tree heathers, on the other hand, respond well to hard cutting and can be renovated. They are usually grown as multi-stemmed trees or large bushes and should be cut back in the first year or so to encourage bushiness. Once established, there is no need to prune other than to keep control of the size of the tree or bush. Do this after flowering. If necessary, it is possible to cut back into old wood.

ESCALLONIA
Escallonia
Evergreen shrubs. Escallonias need little initial training to form bushy shrubs. Once established, they still do not require a great deal of attention but benefit from the removal of some of the oldest wood to stimulate new growth. If they outgrow their position, longer stems, preferably flowered ones, can be cut back to a new shoot or strong bud. They can be

Embothrium coccineum

Eucalyptus gregsoniana

used as formal or informal hedging and can be clipped if necessary. They can be cut hard back for renovation.

EUCALYPTUS
Gum tree
Evergreen trees and shrubs. They are usually grown as single-leader trees. The trunk is kept clear of shoots up to 3m (10ft) for the taller growing specimens. Generally no pruning is required once established, other than to remove dead wood. If they outgrow their space, they can be cut back hard. Some, *E. gunnii* being a common example, can be cut right back, almost to the ground, and then grown as a shrub. The advantage of this is that it produces juvenile foliage, which is much in demand for indoor decorations. This juvenile stage of the foliage can be maintained by regular pollarding so that all the foliage is new.

Euonymus alatus

EUCRYPHIA
Eucryphia
Evergreen trees and shrubs. These are generally grown as single-leader or multi-stemmed trees, or large bushes. Little formative training is needed, as the trees tend to shape up naturally. Similarly, little is required once they are established, although dead wood caused by frost, and sometimes drought, will need to be removed.

EUONYMUS
Spindle
Evergreen and deciduous shrubs. Both require little initial training or established pruning, unless they have outgrown their position. The evergreen *E. fortunei* and its varieties can be trained against a wall, where they will usually grow without support. Tie in or cut out wayward shoots. Variegated forms may produce shoots that have reverted to green, and these should be cut out as soon as they are seen. Euonymus can be cut hard back if renovation is required.

EUPHORBIA
Spurge
A very large genus of trees, shrubs, perennials and annuals. They all exude an irritant sap when cut that can cause problems if it comes in contact with the skin and is very painful indeed if it gets into the eyes. Most of the perennials can be cut back to the ground as they begin to fade, but on shrubby ones, such as *E. characias* and forms, cut back flowered stems as low down as possible after flowering, leaving the new, unflowered shoots to develop. All will regenerate from hard pruning, but once plants get old it is best to replace them.

FAGUS
Beech
Deciduous trees. These large trees generally need no initial or subsequent pruning, other than to remove any dead wood, or to tidy them up if wind breaks one or more of the branches (if these are large a professional may be required to carry out the work).

Fagus sylvatica 'Pendula'

Ficus

Fraxinus ornus

Initial pruning can be used to keep the trunks bare up to about 3m (10ft). They can also be cut very hard and used as hedges. In this compact form, the dead leaves will usually remain on the twigs throughout the winter. Hedges should be trimmed once or twice a year and although slow to recover they can be cut back hard if they become overgrown.

× FATSHEDERA

Evergreen shrub grown for its large glossy leaves. It can be grown as a free-standing shrub, but is usually grown as a wall shrub. Although ivy is one of its parents, it is not self-clinging, so needs tying in to supports as it develops. It produces a number of upright shoots each year, which begin to bow over in the following year, extending the size

PRUNING FORSYTHIA

1 Forsythias flower on old wood so they should not be too drastically pruned or you will not get any flowers. Prune after flowering.

3 Cut out any dead wood, including any stubs left from previous poor pruning. One or two older stems can be taken out completely to rejuvenate the plant.

2 Cut out any congested wood, along with any that crosses other stems, especially if it rubs against or wounds them.

4 The completely pruned plant, now more open and far less crowded. If grown as a hedge, it is usually the inner, unpruned wood that flowers.

of the shrub in an untidy way. Some of these can be tied in to fill gaps but the majority are best removed in the autumn of their first year while they are still upright, cutting them back to their origin. The whole plant can be cut hard back if necessary for renovation.

FICUS
Fig

Evergreen trees grown mainly for their fruit. In colder areas, they are often grown solely for their foliage, as the fruit does not ripen sufficiently. They are most frequently grown as wall shrubs, where they are trained as fans. To prevent them from becoming too rampant, it is best to restrict their roots by creating a bottomless box around them by inserting four paving slabs vertically into the ground. Initial and subsequent pruning is for a fan, although many lose this shape through neglect. Figs can be cut back hard if necessary for renovation.

FORSYTHIA
Forsythia

Deciduous shrubs grown for their spring flowers. Let the plants develop naturally with no initial training. They flower on older wood so any pruning should be after flowering. Cut back some of the oldest wood each year, either to strong new shoots or right to the base. Longer stems can be cut back if the shrub is becoming untidy or outgrowing its space. Forsythia can be grown as a hedge and even if kept cut tight back it produces a surprising number of flowers. It can be cut hard back if renovation is required. *F. suspensa*

can be grown as a wall shrub by tying its pendulous shoots in to wires. Cut out flowered stems to the base of the shoot, tying in replacement ones as they grow.

FRAXINUS
Ash

Deciduous trees grown mainly for their foliage. Little initial training is required. They develop naturally as single-leader trees, although it may be necessary to remove shoots to create a clear trunk up to the desired height. To grow for poles or firewood, develop as multi-stemmed trees and coppice them every few years. Once established, little pruning is required except for taking out dead wood as it appears. Die-back can progressively attack the tree, so it is important to take out any dead wood, cutting into sound wood. They can be cut back hard if necessary. Weeping forms should be trained and pruned as weeping standards.

FREMONTODENDRON
Flannel bush

Evergreen trees or shrubs grown for their foliage and flowers. The foliage and stems are covered with irritating hairs, which can cause damage to skin and, more dangerously, to lungs. They can be grown free-standing but are usually better as wall shrubs. Train with a central leader and tie all side shoots in to a wire framework. The side shoots can also be trained as an espalier so that the pairs of side branches are almost opposite each other and are parallel to the ground. Usually, however, the side branches are tied in to fill the

PRUNING HARDY FUCHSIAS

1 In cooler areas hardy fuchsias are usually killed back to the ground with frosts. They will quickly regenerate the following year.

2 Cut the shrub back almost to ground-level. In warmer areas, where they are not killed by frost, the pruning can be much lighter.

available space and the rest are removed. They flower on the current year's growth, so prune back flowered shoots to a new shoot. They do not respond well to renovation pruning.

FUCHSIA
Fuchsia

Small deciduous or evergreen shrubs, either grown in the open garden or in containers. Some are tender. They are usually grown as shrubs but many are also trained as standards. Initial training consists in pinching out the tips of shoots to promote bushiness. In cold winters they are cut back to the ground by frost, in which case remove the frosted wood back to a bud at the base of the stems in spring. If not frosted, cut back all side shoots to a strong bud. Tender fuchsias should be overwintered under glass to protect them from frost. The main structure is maintained but the shoots are tip-pruned to promote bushiness and to produce an even shape. On standards, keep the trunks clear of shoots.

GARRYA
Silk-tassel bush

Evergreen shrubs grown mainly for their silver winter catkins. No initial training is required, and the bush can be allowed to develop naturally. Once established little pruning is

required except to control it if it overgrows its space. Do this in spring, after flowers have faded. If space is restricted they can be grown as a wall shrub by training in some branches to the wall and removing those that stick out. A bit more pruning is required to keep these in shape, overlapping or congesting shoots should be removed in spring. If renovation is required cut hard back to the main framework.

GENISTA
Broom

Deciduous shrubs grown for their flowers. There is no need for any initial training and established pruning should be kept to a minimum as they dislike being cut back into old wood. After flowering the shrubs can be tidied or kept reasonably compact by cutting back some of the previous year's growth. Renovation is difficult because of the plants' dislike of being cut hard back so replace with new plants if necessary.

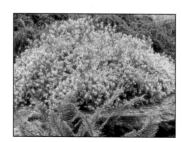

Genista lydia

HAMAMELIS
Witch hazel

Deciduous shrubs grown mainly for their winter flowers. No initial training is required. Pruning can be restricted to removing any dead or rubbing wood, or keeping within bounds. Although the flowers are very attractive in winter, avoid the temptation to cut stems for indoor decoration from all but mature plants as regrowth is usually slow. Although it is rarely necessary, it is possible to renovate with hard pruning but the plant is very slow to regenerate.

HEBE
Hebe

Evergreen shrubs grown for their foliage and flowers. Little initial training is required, and most can be allowed to develop naturally unless their shape becomes unbalanced, in which case remove the offending shoots. Larger varieties can, if left to their own devices, become overlarge and leggy, so regular pruning of flowered shoots after flowering, back to a new shoot, is recommended. Bushes can be kept

Hebe 'Great Orme'

to a rounded shape simply by shearing over every year, just cutting back the flowered wood. Dwarf hummock-forming varieties that are often used as groundcover can also be sheared over to keep them compact. Whipcord types can be left to their own devices. If these become leggy, shear them over to keep them in shape. Hebes can generally be cut back quite hard for renovation purposes.

PRUNING GENISTA

1 Broom is a rather untidy and straggly bush. It is difficult to renovate as it dislikes being cut hard back into old wood.

2 Do not cut back into old wood unless you have to. Dead wood, however, should be removed back to live growth.

3 The only pruning required is to trim back the previous year's growth to keep the plant neater or to control its size.

4 The finished shrub still looks fairly untidy. If it gets out of control, rather than pruning it, plant a new one.

Hedera helix 'Bruder Ingobert'

HEDERA
Ivy
Evergreen climbers used to cover walls and fences. The inconspicuous flowers in late autumn are a valuable food source for bees. Ivies climb by attaching themselves to buildings, trees, fences or anything else that lies in their path. They can also be used as ground cover. For training vertically, tie to canes or peg them down to the base of their supports to make certain that they become attached and climb. On buildings, walls and fences, new shoots should be spread out at the base to create a wide spread. For a wild, gothic look, ivy can be allowed to ramp unchecked over buildings and trees and hang down in curtains, but in other situations it benefits from more control. Little pruning is required other than to cut out shoots that venture above the eaves on buildings. Also cut off any strands that become detached or project forward and spoil the flat plane of the creeper. As ground cover, it needs to be sheared over to about 15cm (6in) every late winter to early spring. It is possible to train ivy over metal or wire frameworks to create a topiary effect. Keep it cut back, close to the former, so that the shape is well defined. Some gardeners dislike the smell of the flowers and the flies and wasps that congregate around them, so

PRUNING HELIANTHEMUM

1 Helianthemums are low-growing, hummocky shrubs. They dislike being cut back hard, but will get straggly if unattended.

2 Cut back the previous year's growth after flowering, being careful not to cut back into old wood, as this will not regrow.

frequently cut them off when they appear in autumn. The best time to prune ivy is in late winter to early spring, but little harm is done by doing it at other times.

HELIANTHEMUM
Rock rose
Low-growing evergreen shrubs grown for their flowers and foliage. Initial training is confined to tip-pruning the shoots to make the plants bush out. Once established, they have a tendency to become straggly and leggy unless they are pruned over once they have flowered. Cut only into the previous year's wood, not into old wood, as this is reluctant to break. Planted en masse, they can be cut with shears, but be careful not to cut into old wood or there will be bald patches. They are difficult to renovate, so start again with new plants.

Helianthemum 'Rhodanthe Carneum'

HELICHRYSUM
Helichrysum
Evergreen shrubs grown mainly for their foliage. The tender shrub *H. petiolare* is widely grown as a container and bedding plant. This should initially be tip-pruned to make it bush out and produce plenty of trailing shoots. If they are constantly pinched out it can be turned into a bushy foliage plant. After overwintering inside, cut out the old stems to new shoots, although it is often best to start again with a new plant. *H. italicum*, the curry plant, is widely grown in the open garden as a small, silver-leaved shrub. Little pruning is required other than to trim over the previous year's growth to keep the plants compact. Many gardeners do not like the yellow flowers and these can be removed before they open, restricting the shrub to a foliage plant. Cut back hard in order to renovate the plant.

HIBISCUS
Hibiscus
Deciduous and evergreen shrubs and perennials grown mainly for their flowers. Initial pruning is required to produce an even framework of branches. Take out weak, crossing and congested stems, and cut back remaining shoots to promote bushiness. Established pruning of hibiscus consists of cutting back the main shoots by about half and side shoots back to a couple of buds in spring. Also take out some of the oldest wood each

year to promote new growth and remove any dead wood as soon as it is evident. Renovation can be achieved by cutting back reasonably hard, work that should preferably be spaced over two or more seasons.

HOYA
Hoya
Evergreen climbers grown for their flowers and foliage. They are tender and in cool climates can only be grown under glass. The sap can cause adverse reactions, so take appropriate precautions when pruning. No initial training is required other than tying the young shoots to their supports. Similarly, there is little established pruning, other than reducing the amount of growth occasionally to prevent congestion. Do this after flowering. Hoyas do not respond well to hard pruning.

HUMULUS
Hop
Perennial climbers grown mainly for their foliage. The bract-covered flowers are often used in interior decorations as well as for brewing beer. They are trained up wires, strings or a wooden framework. They twine but often need guiding initially or they go off sideways and grow up other plants. Twist the young stems clockwise (the opposite way to runner beans) round their supports. Cut to the ground in autumn.

Humulus lupulus 'Aureus'

Hydrangea arborescens

HYDRANGEA
Hydrangea
Deciduous shrubs and climbers grown mainly for their flowers. The main species grown is *H. macrophylla* and its cultivars. No initial pruning is required. Established plants should be pruned in spring by cutting back the previous year's flower heads to a strong bud. Also take out one or two of the oldest stems to regenerate the plant. Other species require minimum pruning. Exceptions are *H. paniculata*, *H. arborescens* and *H. cinerea*, which need to be cut back to a framework of branches by pruning the previous year's growth back to the lowest pair of strong buds in spring. Climbing hydrangeas support themselves by aerial roots but may need tying in initially if they are to cover a wall or fence. Once established they can be vigorous. Cut back all shoots that approach gutters and eaves, and keep clear of windows. They can be cut back hard to regenerate if required.

HYPERICUM
St John's wort
Deciduous and evergreen shrubs grown mainly for their flowers. Most plants require little initial training. Once established, in spring prune back all flowered stems to a new shoot and take out any dead or weak growth. Take out one or two of the oldest stems each year to promote new growth. They can be cut back hard if renovation is required. On ground-cover plants, such as *H. calycinum*, cut out all the previous year's growth. On larger areas this is best done with shears, hedge trimmers or even a strimmer.

Ilex aquifolium 'J.C. van Tol'

ILEX
Holly
Evergreen trees and shrubs grown for their foliage and for their colourful berries. Trees are usually grown as single-leader trees, but are also seen as multi-stemmed trees or large shrubs. Most trees and shrubs can be allowed to develop naturally and little subsequent pruning is necessary. Where grown as topiary or hedge plants, they need to be clipped over once or twice a year to maintain their shape. On trees and shrubs with variegated foliage, cut out any shoots that revert to plain green. Hollies can be cut hard back for renovation (on hedges it is best to spread this over three years).

Jasminum nudiflorum

INDIGOFERA
Indigofera
Deciduous shrubs grown for their flowers and ferny foliage. They require no initial training. Once established, they can be cut to a bud just above ground-level in spring. Left to their own devices, they can grow tall and straggly, in which case they can be cut hard back, again to just above ground-level.

JASMINUM
Jasmine
Evergreen and deciduous climbers and shrubs grown for their flowers (summer varieties usually scented). Initial training consists of tip- pruning the shoots back by half to develop plenty of shoots from the base, and tying these in over as wide an area as possible. Established pruning is restricted to ensuring that the plant does not become congested. Cut out dead wood, which can accumulate, and remove some of the older stems, so that new, rejuvenating growth

Kerria japonica 'Pleniflora'

is produced. If they become over-congested or over-burdened with old wood, it is possible to renovate them by cutting them back drastically to a basic framework. It will take several years to get back to full flowering if treated thus, and so it is best to renovate plants in stages.

KERRIA
Jew's mantle
A single species of deciduous shrub, which is mainly grown for its spring flowers (one cultivar also has variegated foliage). No initial training is required for kerrias. Once established, cut back the flowered wood immediately after flowering has finished, either to a new shoot or to ground-level. Also cut out any unwanted suckers because this shrub can spread. On variegated plants, cut out any shoots that revert to plain green. Kerrias can be renovated by cutting back hard almost to ground-level.

PRUNING WINTER JASMINE

1 *Jasminum nudiflorum* naturally grows into a very tangled bush and if left will soon build up a lot of dead wood.

2 Cut out all the dead wood and thin out the shoots, trying to get an even coverage over the available wall or fence space.

3 A much reduced plant, but there is still some dead wood to be removed. Prune it yearly to keep this under control.

Laburnum × watereri 'Vossii'

KOLKWITZIA
Beauty bush

A single species of deciduous shrub grown for its flowers. No pruning or training is required on planting. When established, it is necessary only to remove some of the oldest stems each year after flowering to rejuvenate the plant constantly. If the plant suckers excessively, remove some or all of those that appear too far from the centre of the plant. Neglected plants can be renovated by cutting out most of the stems to ground-level, leaving just a few young stems.

LABURNUM
Golden rain

Poisonous deciduous trees grown for their flowers. They are often grown as specimens but can also be trained. They will normally develop naturally into single-leader trees, so no initial training is necessary other than the removal of any shoots that appear on the trunk. Once established, pruning should be kept to a minimum except for the removal of dead wood and any shoots that appear below the graft. Laburnums also make good candidates for training over arches, as tunnels or against a wall, where their long, hanging racemes of flowers can be seen to advantage. They can be grown as pleached trees, when established pruning will ensure that they do not become too congested and that shoots are cut back to produce flowering spurs. Against walls, they can be trained as fans, again with spur pruning. Pruning should take place in autumn or early winter, as at any other time the tree may bleed badly. They do not renovate well and so should be replaced if necessary.

LAPAGERIA
Chilean bell flower

One species consisting of an evergreen climber grown for its flowers. Little initial training is needed other than to ensure that it starts to twine up any vertical supports. Once established, very little pruning is required. It does not renovate well so start again, if necessary, with a new plant.

LAURUS
Bay

Evergreen trees or shrubs, either with single or multiple stems. Little initial training is required unless it starts to develop as a multi-stemmed tree in situations where a single-stemmed one is required. In this case, reduce the stems to one and grow on as a feathered tree. It is normal to leave on the lower shoots so that there is hardly any clear trunk. Once established, little pruning is required. If cutting branches for use in the kitchen, take care not to spoil the shape of the tree. Alternatively, just remove leaves from around the tree rather than whole shoots. They can also be developed as clipped forms and are commonly seen as "lollipops" in pots. Plants can be renovated by being cut back to a basic frame, but are slow to regenerate.

LAVANDULA
Lavender

Evergreen shrubs grown for their foliage, flowers and aroma. Once planted, initial training should aim to produce a bushy plant. On established plants, cut back the previous year's growth each spring to within a few buds of the old wood. This can be done with secateurs (pruners) or with shears. Do not cut back into old wood, as this is reluctant to break.

Lavandula angustifolia

Lavatera 'Kew Rose'

After flowering, cut back the long flower stalks. Renovation is difficult and so replace shrubs rather than cutting hard back.

LAVATERA
Tree mallow

Deciduous shrubs grown mainly for their flowers. Little needs to be done in the initial stages, other than to remove any weak growth. Once established, cut back each spring to a shoot or a few buds just above the ground, so that new growth is produced each year. In autumn, reduce the length of all shoots and in windy areas stake the plant, as it can suffer from wind rock. If a hole develops around the base of the trunk, any water that collects there can kill the plant over winter. Replace old plants, as they do not respond well to renovation.

LEYCESTERIA
Himalayan honeysuckle

Deciduous shrubs with hollow, cane-like stems. No initial training or pruning is required. Once established, remove a few of the old stems each year in spring. If the plant begins to sucker too widely, cut these back. If neglected and overgrown, it can be cut hard back almost to ground-level.

Leycesteria formosa

LIGUSTRUM
Privet

Evergreen and semi-deciduous shrubs and trees. They are grown for their foliage and occasionally their flowers but are most frequently seen as hedging. Grown as free-standing shrubs, they need no initial or established pruning, except when green shoots appear on variegated forms. These should be removed as seen. When used as hedging, it is important to promote thick growth right from the base, so cut back newly planted shrubs by half and continue to cut the new growth in a similar manner each year until the hedge is formed. Once formed, trim two or three times a year, ensuring that it is not allowed to grow away. If it does become overgrown, it can be cut back severely, as can free-standing shrubs.

LIQUIDAMBAR
Sweet gum

Deciduous trees grown for their foliage, especially the autumn colour. They are grown as a central-leader tree, which develops naturally, so there is little initial training or pruning apart from ensuring that a short trunk is kept clear. Once established, no pruning is necessary.

LIRIODENDRON
Tulip tree

Deciduous trees grown for their flowers and distinctively shaped foliage. This is a relatively easy tree to grow as far as the pruning is concerned, as there is very little to do. It is grown as a single-leader tree, the trunk cleared of shoots up to the desired height, usually about 2.5m (8ft). Once established, it is best to leave it alone, except for removing any dead or damaged wood.

Liquidambar styraciflua

Lonicera × brownii

Magnolia denudata 'Forrest's Pink'

Malus × schiedeckeri 'Hillieri'

LONICERA
Honeysuckle

Deciduous and evergreen climbers and shrubs. The climbers are the most frequently grown, but a lot of shrubby forms are available. Climbers should be trained to their supports so that they cover the maximum available space. If they are left unpruned, eventually the base will become bare and dead wood will accumulate in a top-heavy plant. It is best to prune a little each year after flowering, cutting back flowered stems to just a couple of buds. Take out any dead wood. They can be cut back hard to within 60–90cm (2–3ft) of the base, but will take a while to reach maximum flowering potential again. Bushes should be pruned after flowering, cutting out a few of the oldest stems and any weak growth to increase vigour. Any remaining longer shoots can be shortened to a new shoot to keep them in shape and within bounds, as some species can become rather leggy. Cut hard back to renovate. *L. nitida* is used as a hedging plant and should be treated in the same way as privet hedging. It can be cut back to near the ground to renovate.

MAGNOLIA
Magnolia

Deciduous and evergreen trees and shrubs. The trees are either single- or multi-stemmed. Initial pruning is usually aimed at creating the former. Do not remove lower side shoots to clear the trunk until after the leader is well developed. Multi-stemmed plants can be left to their own devices, but it may eventually be necessary to take off some of the lower laterals. Most can be left unpruned, once they are established. They can be renovated, but take it gently, a few branches at a time over a period of years. *M. grandiflora* is usually grown against a wall. Allow the leader to develop and tie in the side shoots to wires, maintaining as even a spread as possible. Once developed, cut back the shoots on the main branches to a couple of leaves after flowering. Shrubby forms should be allowed to develop unpruned according to their natural habitat. Once established, prune as little as possible.

MAHONIA
Oregon grape

Evergreen shrubs that are grown for their foliage and flowers. On the more vigorous species, cut out one or two of the oldest shoots from the base every few years. Otherwise, little pruning is required. If they get leggy or misshapen, cut back shoots after flowering to a strong shoot or bud. All can be cut hard back, but may take a while to get back to flowering size afterwards. *M. aquifolium* produces lots of suckers and tends to form a thicket. It can be kept in check by removing the perimeter ones or cutting them back every two or three years in order to produce fresh growth.

MALUS
Crab apple

Deciduous trees grown for their ornamental and edible fruit. Ornamental crab apples are relatively easy to prune. They are grown as central-leader trees. They can generally be left to their own devices, except that the trunk should be cleared of shoots to the required height, usually around 1.2–2m (4–6ft). If the leader is lost, either grow the tree as a multi-stemmed bush or train in a new leader. Once established, little pruning is required. Some varieties produce many suckers or vertical shoots rising from the main limbs. These should be removed, along with any crossing or rubbing wood. Any dead or diseased wood should also be removed. Pruning should take place in the winter.

MYRTUS
Myrtle

Deciduous or evergreen shrubs grown for their foliage and flowers. No initial training or pruning is required, and little is necessary once they are established unless they outgrow

their allotted space, in which case longer shoots can be trimmed back to within the shrub in spring. It can be renovated by cutting hard back, preferably over several years.

NANDINA
Sacred bamboo

A single species of evergreen shrub, grown mainly for its berries. No initial training is necessary. Once established, it can be left to its own devices, although the removal of some of the older wood each year in spring will help to stimulate the plant. Complete renovation can be carried out by cutting the plant to near ground-level, preferably over several years.

NERIUM
Oleander

Evergreen shrubs or small trees that are grown for their attractive foliage and flowers. In cool climates, they must be grown as container plants and overwintered inside, in a glasshouse or conservatory. Be warned that the sap is toxic and should not be swallowed. It can also cause skin reactions, so take adequate precautions when pruning or handling. There is no initial training for shrubs except to tip-prune them to make them bush out. In the open, they can more or less be left to their own devices but they will need to be cut back if in containers. Reduce all flowered shoots by about half after flowering and cut back any side shoots to just a couple of leaves. Oleanders can be grown as standards. Shrubs can be renovated by cutting hard back to a basic framework, but may take time to recover.

Mahonia aquifolium 'Apollo'

Malus

THINNING OUT OLEARIA

1 Olearias generally need very little pruning, although they can become rather straggly, in which case they can be cut back.

2 If the shrub has completely outgrown its position, it can be cut back hard. It will usually recover from such treatment.

Parthenocissus tricuspidata

Passiflora 'Amethyst'

NOTHOFAGUS
Southern beech
Evergreen and deciduous trees that can grow to enormous size. They are generally grown as single-stemmed trees although they sometimes develop with more than one trunk. These can be left to grow as multi-stemmed trees, but if this occurs as the result of the loss of the leader at some height, this may prove a weak point in the tree. In this case, a new leader should be formed and any rivals removed. Once established, the trees can be left to look after themselves.

OLEARIA
Daisy bush
Evergreen shrubs grown for their foliage and flowers. Initial training is confined to shortening the young shoots to promote bushiness. Once established, there is no need for pruning, although they may need cutting back if they get leggy or outgrow their allotted space. Taking out some of the oldest wood every year or so should help to keep the plant vigorous. It can be renovated by cutting back hard into old wood.

OSMANTHUS
Osmanthus
Evergreen shrubs grown for their foliage and scented flowers. Initial training is generally not required, and the shrubs can be allowed to develop naturally. However, they can be tip-pruned to make them bush out if necessary. Little established pruning is required other than keeping the bushes within bounds. Any pruning should be done in spring (spring-flowering species immediately after flowering). They can be cut hard back for renovation purposes.

PAEONIA
Peony
Shrubs and herbaceous plants grown for their flowers and foliage. The shrubby ones are generally referred to as tree peonies. No initial training or pruning is required. Once established, little pruning is required except that they should be deadheaded, cutting back the flowered stem to just above a leaf or shoot. They make rather ungainly shrubs. Removing some of the older growth every few years promotes new, bushier growth. This can be done in autumn or early winter. They can be renovated by cutting hard back but are slow to regenerate, so a yearly routine of removing older material is preferable. Herbaceous plants should not be cut back until the winter, as their foliage often takes on autumn tints and the seed pods are rather attractive.

PARTHENOCISSUS
Virginia creeper
Deciduous climbers that are grown for their foliage, especially for their autumn coloration. They can be vigorous. Initial training consists of training the shoots to spread out as far as possible. Once they reach the wall or support, they are self-clinging, so rarely need any further supports. Established pruning can be restricted to making certain that the climbers stay within bounds. Cut them back when they reach the tops of walls to prevent them from getting into gutters and eaves and under tiles. Also cut them back around windows and vents. Do this in winter. If necessary, they can generally be cut back hard to within 1m (3ft) of the ground for renovation.

PASSIFLORA
Passion flower
Evergreen or semi-evergreen climbers, most of which are not hardy. In cooler areas, *P. caerulea* is the main species grown. It has tendrils and is self-clinging but should be grown over a suitable framework, either against a wall or fence, or over a structure. Initial training consists of spreading out the young shoots to cover as wide an area as possible. Tip-prune these to encourage more shoots to develop. Tie in any wayward shoots. Once developed, cut back flowered shoots to within a few leaves or buds of the main branch. Otherwise, just remove any weak, dead or congested growth unless it is necessary to cut back longer stems to keep the plant within bounds. They do not respond well to hard cutting back, so replant rather than renovate.

PRUNING OSMANTHUS

1 *Osmanthus delavayii* generally needs no pruning, either initially or when established, other than the removal of dead wood.

2 If the shrub is getting too large for its position, then some of the longer shoots can be cut back. Any wayward shoots can also be removed.

3 Dead, diseased or damaged wood should be removed when it is seen. Any pruning should be in spring, after flowering.

PAULOWNIA
Foxglove tree

Deciduous trees grown for their foliage and flowers. Initial training should be directed towards developing a single-leader tree, although, if you prefer, it can be left to develop as a multi-stemmed tree or shrub. If a single trunk is desired, train a single leader, creating a clear trunk up to 1.2–2m (4–6ft) by removing shoots as they appear. Once established, there is no need for pruning in either the tree or shrub form. Sometimes suckers appear and these should be removed. Renovation is not easy and it is better to replant in the unlikely event of this being necessary.

PEROVSKIA
Russian sage

Deciduous shrubs grown for their foliage and flowers. After planting cut back to within one or two buds of the previous year's growth. Continue to do this throughout the plant's life, cutting it back each spring, so that the framework of the plant is

Perovskia 'Blue Spire'

kept relatively low to the ground. Every few years, remove some of the oldest basal structure to promote vigour.

PHILADELPHUS
Mock orange

Deciduous shrubs grown mainly for their fragrant flowers. They shoot mainly from the base in the form of a stool, so no initial training or pruning is required. Once established, flowered stems can be cut back to a suitable new shoot or to the base. Remove a

few of the oldest shoots each year to promote new growth and vigour. Carry this out after flowering. *P. microphyllus* is an exception, as little or no pruning is required. Renovation is best carried out as a continuous process, but if a shrub does become overgrown or neglected, cut out most of the oldest wood to ground-level and shorten newer shoots by about half their length.

PHLOMIS
Phlomis

Evergreen shrubs grown for their foliage and flowers. Be warned: the "dust" from the leaves and stems of some species can cause an allergic reaction, so wear a mask when pruning. No initial training or pruning is generally required. Little pruning is required after the shrubs are established other than the removal of the flower stems back to leaves or shoots. This can be done in autumn. They may need shaping if they outgrow their position. Cut back overlong shoots to a suitable shoot within the bush. This is best done in spring. The more tender species, such as *P. italica*, benefit from the removal of frosted wood in spring. Renovate neglected plants by cutting back hard to a basic framework.

PHOTINIA
Photinia

Deciduous and evergreen shrubs and trees grown mainly for their foliage. Generally, there is no need for any initial training and pruning unless you want to train

PRUNING PHLOMIS

1 Phlomis may lose its leaves in the winter, but still break again from old wood. Wood that has been severely damaged by frost may be killed and should be cut out.

2 Wait until the buds break to see where to cut back to. If a bud breaks from a defoliated stem, there is no need to cut back unless it is too long or misplaced.

it as a standard. Once established, no pruning is required, though it is possible to enhance the spring colour of the foliage by cutting back the tips of the shoots to a strong bud. This should be carried out in early spring. For neglected plants, cut hard back to a basic framework. Photinias can be grown as a hedge and can be trimmed two or three times a year; this is necessary less often for an informal hedge.

PHYGELIUS
Phygelius

Two evergreen shrubs or subshrubs grown for their flowers. No initial training or pruning is required, although it helps to tip-prune to stimulate bushy growth. Every spring, cut out any frosted wood back to a shoot and remove some of the old wood to a basal shoot or bud. If neglected, they can become

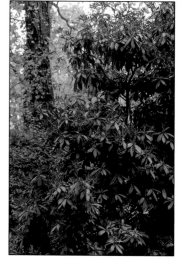

Photinia × *fraseri*

PRUNING PEROVSKIA

1 Perovskias produce a lot of old flowering growth each year. It is advisable to cut this back to a low framework.

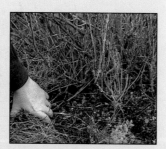

2 Since perovskias are usually grown in herbaceous borders, clear away the remains of any herbaceous material from around the plant.

3 Cut the old flowering stems right down to one or two buds of the previous year's growth, which should be just above the ground.

4 As the plants age, they will produce knobbly stools, some of which can be removed in order to stimulate new growth.

Pieris japonica

Potentilla fruticosa

Prunus 'Shirotae'

very straggly and leggy, so try to renovate at least part of the plant each year. If in need of serious renovation, cut all the stems back almost to ground-level.

PIERIS
Pieris
Evergreen shrubs grown for their young foliage and flowers. They need little or no formative training. Generally, there is little need for pruning once the shrub becomes established. If necessary, cut out all frosted wood in spring. Remove the flower heads after the flowers have faded. Renovation can be achieved by cutting hard back to a basic framework.

PITTOSPORUM
Pittosporum
Evergreen shrubs and trees grown for their foliage. Very little initial training or pruning is required except to ensure that trees grow with a single stem. Do not clear the trunk of shoots as it looks better if clothed to the ground. Little subsequent pruning is required unless it is to shape it or keep it within bounds, in which case cut stems back inside the plant in the spring. Renovation, if necessary, can usually be achieved by cutting back hard to a basic framework.

POLYGONUM
Russian vine
Vigorous deciduous climber. They can grow very large, so

need strong supports. Avoid growing through dead trees as the weight and windage could topple the tree. The only initial training involved is to lead and tie in the shoots to their supports, spreading them out so a good coverage is achieved. Generally, the vine becomes such a tangled mass that pruning is impractical. The only thing that may need doing is to cut back the outer limits of the plant to control its spread. This can be done with shears or even a hedge trimmer. If renovation is necessary, reduce the whole plant to within 60–90cm (2–3ft) of the ground to restart it.

POPULUS
Poplar
Deciduous trees mainly grown for their foliage. These are fast-growing and often large trees that are unsuitable for most small gardens. They are all trained as a central-leader tree. Most look best with clear trunks up to 2–3m (6–10ft), but often the wounds left by removing branches will cause more to appear. They should be rubbed out as soon as they appear. Any pruning should be done in early winter, as poplars bleed less when dormant. Once developed, there is little need for further pruning, except for removal of dead branches. Any large-scale work should be left to specialist

tree surgeons. Some poplars produce suckers that should be removed. Some species are very prone to canker, and it is best to avoid pruning these so that there are no open wounds through which the disease can enter. Poplars do not renovate very well.

POTENTILLA
Cinquefoil
Deciduous shrubs grown for their flowers and foliage. Little formative pruning is required, although lightly tipping back the shoots produces a bushier plant. Once established, remove any branches that become overlong and take out one or two of the oldest stems each year in spring to renew the shrub's vigour. Clip over the plant after flowering to tidy it up. Constant renewal is better than cutting the whole shrub back at once. If a plant has become very untidy, it is best to replace it with a new plant.

PRUNUS
Ornamental cherry
Deciduous and evergreen trees and shrubs grown mainly for their flowers but also for their bark and (in deciduous types) autumn foliage. In general, prune deciduous types as little as possible. For initial training, prune as central-leader trees with a clear trunk, or as weeping standards. Suckers may appear from the roots, often some distance from the trunk. Remove these from below ground. Water shoots will often appear on the trunks, especially from around old pruning wounds. Remove these as well by rubbing out as they appear. Any grafted varieties should have any shoots that appear from below the graft removed. Other than that, avoid any pruning unless essential. Evergreens are treated in a similar way, although some can be severely pruned into topiary or hedges.

PRUNING PITTOSPORUM

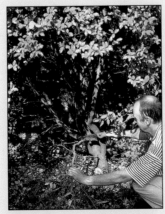

1 Pittosporums need little pruning. Any dead or, as here, damaged branches should be cut back to a suitable point.

2 Cut out any multiple stems that cause congestion or badly rub against other stems. These can be cut right back to the ground.

3 Cut out any over-vigorous shoots that spoil the shape of the shrub or tree. Also cut out long shoots if they are outgrowing its space.

PYRACANTHA
Firethorn

Evergreen shrubs grown mainly for their berries. Be warned that they are armed with vicious thorns which can penetrate deeply. Wear thick gloves and some form of arm protection when pruning. Pyracanthas can be trained either as free-standing shrubs or as wall shrubs, the latter generally being preferred (especially under windows, as the thorns make them a burglar deterrent). Free-standing shrubs need little attention either initially or when established, except for tidying up if necessary by cutting back overlong stems. Wall-trained shrubs are usually trained against wires, either informally by tying branches in to the wires as and when gaps occur, or more formally by training either as an espalier (with horizontal branches on either side of a central stem) or as a fan. Once established, cut shoots back to a few buds in summer to keep the plant compact against the wall and to prevent overcrowding. They do not always renovate well from hard pruning and it may be better to replace them if necessary. They can be grown as compact, thorny hedges, which need pruning two or three times a year to keep them in shape.

PYRUS
Pear

Deciduous trees grown for their fruit, and for their foliage and flowers. Among the decorative varieties, one of the most popular is the silver foliage form, especially in its weeping variety (*Pyrus salicifolia* 'Pendula'). The trees are all grown as central-leader trees and should have clear trunks. Weeping varieties may need staking initially to encourage the trunk to grow upright, as they sometimes have a tendency to lean and become lop-sided. Once developed, most pears need little pruning other than the removal of dead or diseased wood. Fireblight, a disease causing blackish-brown leaves, can be a problem. Cut out the affected wood and sterilize the tools before using them again to prevent spread of the disease.

Quercus frainetto

QUERCUS
Oak

Deciduous and evergreen trees grown for their foliage and general shape. Most oak trees are likely to develop naturally into central-leader trees unless they are damaged in some way. Remove any growth on their trunks up to the level of the desired lowest branches, usually around 2.5–3m (8–10ft). Very little pruning is required except to remove dead branches, especially from very mature trees, but this is often best left to a specialist tree surgeon, as is cutting back overgrown trees. Oaks can be renovated quite hard but will take a long time to recover their normal shape. Any pruning should take place in winter.

RHODOCHITON

Deciduous perennial climbers. Initial training is confined to pinching out the tips to promote

Rhododendron 'Loder's White'

bushiness and spreading the stems wide to produce good coverage. They should be provided with vertical supports such as twigs or strings, as they have leaf stalks that enable them to climb. Once established, no pruning is required other than the removal of dead material. They are relatively short-lived, so replace rather than renovate plants.

RHODODENDRON
Rhododendron, azalea

Evergreen and deciduous shrubs and trees grown for their foliage and flowers. Generally they need little initial training or pruning but are left to develop their natural habit. If necessary, shorten overlong branches to improve the overall shape. Once established, they can be left to their own devices, with no work necessary other than the removal of dead wood. Most benefit from deadheading after flowering, but this can be impractical on large

Ribes sanguineum

shrubs. Some produce suckers and these should be removed, especially on grafted specimens. Most are not easy to renovate, with the exception of *R. ponticum*, which will reshoot even if cut back almost to ground-level.

RHUS
Sumach

Deciduous trees or shrubs grown for their foliage (especially the autumn tints) and flower heads. There is no need for initial training unless you want to grow the plant as a tree. In this case, choose a strong stem and train it as a central leader with a clear trunk up to 1.2m (4ft) or so. There is very little subsequent pruning required except for the removal of suckers from below ground level. These can be produced in large quantities, causing serious problems when plants are neglected. Sumachs can be pruned hard back almost to ground-level every spring to produce especially good foliage. They can be renovated in the same way.

RIBES
Currant

Deciduous shrubs grown for their flowers and foliage or for their fruit. Decorative forms need little initial training. Once established, just remove one or two stems of the oldest wood every year after flowering. *R. speciosum* is often trained flat against a wall or fence. It can be grown either with branches tied in at random to fill the available space or trained in a systematic way as a fan. Renovation is best carried out by regular removal of a few old stems, but they can be cut back hard.

DEADHEADING RHODODENDRONS

1 Rhododendrons generally need little pruning, but keep them neat by pinching out dead flower-heads.

2 Take them out carefully so that the surrounding buds, carrying next year's flowers, are not damaged.

PRUNING SANTOLINA

1 Santolinas can become very straggly and untidy-looking. It is not always possible to renovate them successfully.

2 However, if there are plenty of new shoots in the middle of the bush, then it is possible to prune them hard in the spring.

3 The pruned shrub showing all the new growth waiting to develop. If there are no suitable shoots, dig out the plant and replace it.

Sambucus racemosa

ROSA
Rose
Deciduous shrubs and climbers grown for their flowers. These are dealt with in detail under *Roses*.

ROSMARINUS
Rosemary
Evergreen shrubs grown for their foliage and flowers. No formative training or pruning is required. Once established, no pruning is required except to cut back any overlong shoots. Young shoots can be pinched out for culinary purposes, but spread this around the bush so that the gaps do not show. They can become aged and rather scrawny, in which case it is best to replace them rather than to attempt renovation. This lax growth can to a certain extent be avoided by cutting back the new growth lightly each year to keep the plant compact.

RUBUS
Bramble
Deciduous shrubs grown for their flowers or winter stems. Fruiting forms are dealt with under *Fruit Trees*. Species that are grown for the colour of their winter stems should be cut back to the ground in late spring. For those grown for their flowers, cut out the flowered wood after flowering back to a new shoot. At the same time, remove one or two of the oldest shoots to keep the plant growing vigorously.

SALIX
Willow
Deciduous shrubs and trees grown for their foliage, flowers (catkins) or winter stems. For general use, they can be allowed to develop naturally without any initial training (unless planted as a "living fence", in which case stems can be woven). Once established, little or no pruning is required unless they are to be pollarded or coppiced. For colourful winter stems, the young shoots are usually cut right back in spring. For living fences individual wands are rooted and then woven into the desired shape. Usually side-shoots that develop are cut back to a single bud in the autumn, so that the shape and pattern of the woven wands is still apparent. Willow can be cut back hard for renovation. Small weeping varieties should have their branches thinned each year and

Salix repens

the remaining ones cut back by about half to an outward-facing bud. Large weeping varieties should be initially trained and pruned as a single-leader tree with a clear trunk up to about 2m (6ft). Once established, little pruning is required.

SALVIA
Sage
Evergreen shrubs grown for their foliage and flowers. Prune back the shoots on planting to promote bushiness. Once established, cut back the previous year's growth to a couple of buds in the spring. Also in spring, any dead wood in *S. officinalis* should be removed. If used for culinary purposes, remove leaves and stems throughout the shrub rather than making one area bare. Sage can be cut hard back for renovation, but it is better to keep it under control in the first place.

SAMBUCUS
Elder
Deciduous shrubs grown for their foliage and flowers. Most elders can be allowed to develop naturally for the first two or three years. Thereafter, treatment varies depending on what you want from the plant. For those grown for foliage effect, cut back all the stems to a framework just above soil level in early spring before growth starts. This will promote large and colourful foliage. If

grown for flowers, remove only the oldest stems, cutting back the younger shoots to about half their length. If left unpruned for a couple of years, dead wood starts to accumulate, and this should be removed. They generally respond well to renovative pruning, but very old plants are best replaced.

SANTOLINA
Santolina
Evergreen shrubs grown for their foliage. Newly planted specimens should have their shoots reduced to encourage bushiness. Once developed, clip over in spring to keep the plant compact. In summer, it produces yellow flowers which many gardeners feel spoil the foliage effect. They can be removed as soon as the flower buds start to appear. If the flowers are allowed, trim them off in autumn once they have faded. Straggly plants are best replaced, as they do not respond well to renovation.

Santolina pinnata subsp. *neapolitana*

SCHIZOPHRAGMA
Schizophragma

Deciduous climbers grown for flowers and foliage. They are best grown on walls or strong fences but can be grown over other supports, including trees. They have aerial roots and so are self-supporting, but stems do need to be led to their support from the planting position, which should be well away from the wall (at least 45cm/18in). Spread out the shoots as much as possible to produce good coverage. Once established, little pruning is required although it is a sensible precaution to prevent them from entering gutters, eaves and vents as well as keeping them away from roofs. Take out one or two of the oldest stems each year after flowering to promote constant renewal.

SKIMMIA
Skimmia

Evergreen shrubs grown for their foliage, flowers and berries. They rarely need much pruning other than to remove any dead, damaged or diseased wood. Any pruning is cosmetic. Cut out overlong branches that upset the balance of the bush. It forms a compact bush and rarely needs trimming, but if you do, use secateurs (pruners) rather than shears, which will cut through the large leaves.

SOLANUM
Potato vine

Deciduous shrubs and climbers grown mainly for their flowers.

Sorbus

Spiraea × arguta

Syringa × josiflexa

The sap can cause skin problems so take appropriate precautions when pruning. Climbers can be grown against any kind of support but look particularly good against walls. They are not self-clinging so will need to be tied into wires. Prune back shoots on planting to encourage bushiness, then spread these out to get wide coverage. Tie in shoots as they develop. In spring, prune back side shoots to two or three buds to form a framework of stems. Remove any dead wood. Cut back the oldest stems each year to promote renovation. Drastic renovation is usually unsuccessful. If old, straggly or overgrown, replace with a new plant.

SORBUS
Rowan

Deciduous trees and shrubs grown for their foliage, flowers and fruit. Formative training and pruning consists of growing them as central-leader trees, a habit they generally assume naturally. Clear the trunk to 1.2–2m (4–6ft). Once established, little pruning is

necessary, except to keep the base of the trunk clear of any suckers. Rowans are difficult to renovate, so replace if necessary.

SPIRAEA
Spiraea

Deciduous or evergreen shrubs grown for their foliage and flowers. Generally, no formative pruning is required. Once established, cut back flowered stems to the next shoot after flowering. Also remove one or two of the oldest shoots each year to promote continuing vigour. Renovation is best achieved by constant renewals as above.

STEPHANANDRA
Stephanandra

Deciduous shrubs grown for their foliage, especially in autumn, and flowers. No initial pruning is required and established pruning is restricted to removing a few of the oldest stems each year after flowering to achieve constant renewal. Stephanandra can sucker, and it may be necessary to remove some suckers annually to prevent the shrub spreading. Renovation can

be achieved by cutting back the shrub hard to almost ground-level in early spring.

STEPHANOTIS
Bridal wreath

Evergreen tropical climbers that are mainly grown under glass in cooler countries. Initial training consists of cutting back shoots to promote bushness. Once established, thin out some of the older wood occasionally to prevent congestion, and cut back any overlong stems if necessary. They do not respond well to hard pruning, so replant rather than cutting back hard.

SYRINGA
Lilac

Deciduous shrubs grown for their flowers. Some form a typical shrub shape while others develop more like small multi-stemmed trees. No initial training is required unless the shrub becomes misshapen. Once established, the main task is to deadhead if you can easily reach all the faded flowers. Take care not to damage the new buds behind the flower head. Also remove suckers as they appear. If it becomes necessary, lilacs can be cut hard back for renovation purposes.

TAMARIX
Tamarisk

Airy deciduous shrubs and trees grown for their flowers and feathery foliage. Initial pruning consists of pruning back shoots to promote bushiness, both in its first and next two seasons. Once established, cut back flowered stems to a strong shoot. Do this after flowering, except with late-flowering varieties, which should be pruned in spring. They can be renovated by cutting back hard to a basic framework.

PRUNING SKIMMIA

1 Skimmias do not usually need any pruning and are spoilt if tightly pruned. However, they do occasionally have dead stems that need to be removed.

2 (*right*) Cut these stems out, along with any damaged shoots, back to sound wood.

3 The shrubs are usually well balanced, but if there are any wayward shoots, remove these as well, cutting back into the bush.

Tilia platyphyllos

THYMUS
Thyme
Low-growing shrubs grown for their foliage and flowers as well as for culinary purposes. No initial training is required. Once established, cut back flowered stems, but do not cut back into old wood. If picking for the kitchen, only cut the new growth or gaps will appear. Some of those with decorative foliage may well have shoots that revert back to the original green. Cut these out as soon as they appear. If plants get too old and straggly, replace them, as cutting back hard is seldom successful.

TILIA
Lime
Deciduous trees grown for their foliage and flowers. Their size means they are usually best in large gardens, unless they are pleached. Formative training is as a single-leader tree, with a trunk cleared of shoots and branches to about 2–3m (6–10ft). Little subsequent pruning is required unless there is a problem with the tree, when professional tree surgeons should be called in. The trees can be easily pleached to provide screens or covered walkways. Renovation should always be carried out by professionals.

TRACHELOSPERMUM
Star jasmine
Evergreen climbers grown for their foliage and flowers. They are twiners and should be provided with a vertical support. Initial

Trachelospermum asiaticum

training consists of spreading out the shoots so that the whole of the support will be covered, and tying them in to get them started. Little or no pruning is required once established. Cut back shoots in spring by half for renovation. Extremely overgrown plants are best replaced.

ULMUS
Elm
Deciduous trees grown for their foliage and shape. These are mainly very big trees and any serious pruning needs to be undertaken by a professional tree surgeon. Initially they should be trained and pruned, if necessary, as single-leader trees, clearing the trunk from 2–3m (6–10ft) and maintaining a balanced shape. Little further pruning is required. Renovation should be undertaken by professionals.

VIBURNUM
Viburnum
Deciduous and evergreen shrubs grown for their flowers, foliage and (sometimes) fruit. All need little initial pruning The deciduous winter-flowering types, such as *V. × bodnantense*, should be

Viburnum opulus 'Xanthocarpum'

pruned once established by removing some of the oldest growth from the base each year in spring. Others require the minimum of pruning, although those that sucker or layer should have any suckers removed to prevent the shape of the plant being compromised. Most can be cut back hard for renovation purposes. *V. tinus* can be trained as an attractive standard.

VINCA
Periwinkle
Evergreen shrubs that are grown for their foliage and flowers as well as for ground cover. Initial training is unnecessary, but once established it is likely to be necessary to cut back long shoots to keep the plant compact and to prevent them rooting outside their allotted space. Ground cover can be sheared or strimmed over to keep it neat and compact to the ground. Those grown through hedges can be cut back when the hedge is cut. Alternatively, reduce long, arching stems as necessary. Renovation consists of cutting plants hard back to the ground.

VITIS
Vine
Deciduous climbers grown for their foliage and/or fruit. The decorative forms need to be supported by a strong trellis or pergola, although they can also be trained through trees. Cut back the original shoots to

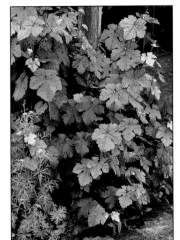

Vitis vinifera 'Purpurea'

encourage more to grow, and tie the resulting shoots in to the support to ensure maximum coverage. Continue to tie in as the plant develops. Once the space is covered, cut back all side shoots to one or two buds each winter. If the vines are particularly vigorous, it may be necessary to repeat this in summer. If they are grown solely for their leaves, remove flowers as they appear. Overgrown plants can be renovated by cutting back hard, even right to the base if necessary.

WEIGELA
Weigela
Deciduous shrubs grown mainly for their flowers. Formative pruning is not generally required. Once the plant is established and starts flowering, cut back the flowered stems after flowering to a strong shoot. If the shrub becomes misshapen with overlong stems, reduce these in length. In spring, cut out one or two of the oldest stems to promote constant rejuvenation. On variegated and coloured foliage forms, cut out any stems that bear plain green leaves. Renovate by cutting back hard almost to ground-level.

WISTERIA
Wisteria
Deciduous climbers grown for flowers and foliage. For further details of pruning and training, see *Ornamental Climbers and Wall Shrubs*.

Wisteria floribunda

Glossary

Acclimatization The need to allow new trees and shrubs to get used to cooler or moister conditions if they have been grown under cover.

Adventitious buds Dormant buds waiting to be stimulated into growth. They frequently cannot be seen.

Aerial roots Roots that emerge from trunks or other stems above ground.

Alternate Said of leaves or buds when they are not directly opposite one another on a stem, but staggered.

Apex The tip of a stem or shoot.

Axil The upper angle that a leaf stalk makes with the stem.

Axillary buds Buds that are formed in the axils, i.e. between the leaf stalk and the stem.

Bare-rooted Plants that are bought or otherwise acquired that are not in a container, and have had the soil removed from their roots.

Basal Leaves or shoots growing at the base of a plant.

Blind shoots Shoots that have failed to produce a flower.

Bracts Petal-like modified leaves that often appear around a flower. Frequently coloured.

Branch leader The main shoot of a branch that is increasing its length.

Break Shoots, leaves or blossom starting to grow from the buds.

Canopy The main part of the tree above the trunk.

Central leader The main, central shoot of a tree or shrub.

Chainsaw A motor-driven saw for cutting through large branches or trunks.

Climber A shrub, perennial or annual that grows through other plants, or needs walls or a framework for support.

Coppicing Regular cutting back to ground or near ground-level of trees and shrubs, done to stimulate new growth.

Crown The main part of the tree above the trunk.

Cultivar A variation originating in cultivation of a wild plant.

Deadheading The removal of fading or dead flowers or their resulting seed pods.

Deciduous Plants in which the leaves die and fall during their dormant period.

Defoliation Loss or removal of leaves.

Die-back The dying of shoots or other wood from either the tip or point of cutting.

Dormancy A period when a plant is inactive in winter.

Dwarfing rootstock Rootstock that produces small trees.

Epicormic shoots Shoots that appear on the stem, often on the trunk of mature trees as a result of wounds.

Evergreen A plant that does not lose its leaves at the end of its growing season.

Fastigiate Describing narrow trees and shrubs with almost vertical branches.

Feathered Trees with branches or shoots on either side of a main trunk.

Feathered maiden A one-year-old tree with a main stem and side shoots.

Framework The permanent structure of branches.

Graft Joining one type of plant on to another plant's rootstock.

Graft union The junction between the top (scion) and the bottom (rootstock) of a grafted plant.

Internode The piece of shoot between two nodes, i.e. between two side shoots, leaves or buds.

Lateral Side shoot.

Leader A main stem.

Long-arm pruners Secateurs (pruners) on a long pole that can be operated from the lower end while reaching up into trees.

Long-handled pruners Secateurs (pruners) that have long handles for cutting thicker stems.

Maiden A tree in its first year.

Maiden whip A tree in its first year without as yet any side shoots.

Mulch A ground-covering material to conserve moisture and prevent weed growth.

Multi-stemmed A tree or shrub with more than one main stem or trunk.

Petiole A leaf stalk.

Pinching out To prune by pinching out a soft shoot between finger and thumb.

Pleaching Training adjacent trees so that their branches are interwoven to form a screen.

Pollarding Cutting back all of the branches or shoots of a tree from the top of its trunk.

Pot-bound A container-grown plant in which the roots have outgrown the available space and are wound round each other.

Prostrate Growing along the ground.

Pruning saw A special saw designed specifically for pruning.

Pyramid trees Small trees in the shape of a cone or round pyramid.

Rambler A climbing plant that scrambles through other plants.

Repeat flowering Of a plant that has more than one flowering period.

Replacement shoot A strong shoot that is used to replace the one being removed.

Reversion A process whereby variegated plants produce plain green leaves.

Ripe wood Wood that has hardened.

Root-bound A container-grown plant in which the roots have outgrown the available space in the container and are wound round each other.

Rootball The collection of roots, still with their soil, as found in a container or when a plant is dug up.

Rootstock The rooted section of a grafted plant.

Rubbing out Removal of soft shoots by rubbing with the hand.

Secateurs (pruners) Hand tools that are somewhat like strong scissors for pruning thin stems.

Scion The upper part of a grafted plant, from which the plant takes most of its character.

Secondary growth Late summer growth after pruning.

Semi-evergreen A plant that retains some of its leaves while discarding others during its dormant period.

Semi-standard A tree that is half-way between a bush tree and a full standard. The clear trunk is usually about 1.2m (4ft).

Shears A scissor-like cutting tool for trimming hedges.

Side shoot A shoot that appears on the side of a more major stem.

Snag A short length of stem between a bud and a pruning cut.

Standard (1) A full-size tree usually with a clear trunk. (2) A shrub grafted on to a single stem to appear like a miniature tree.

Stool A cluster of stems all rising from the same place at ground-level. Coppicing often produces them.

Stopping Pinching out a shoot to make it branch out.

Stub The remaining portion of a shoot when the rest has been cut off.

Sub-lateral A side shoot on a shoot that is already a side shoot itself.

Sucker Shoots that arise from around the base of a plant or from its roots, often from the rootstock of a grafted plant.

Terminal The tip of a shoot.

Thinning Reducing the number of shoots or spurs.

Tip-pruning Removing the tip of a shoot to make it branch out.

Topiary A decorative way of shaping a bush.

Trunk The main stem of a tree.

Variegated Foliage consisting of more than one colour.

Water shoots Quick-growing shoots that can appear on the trunks of certain trees, often stimulated by wounds.

Weeping Trees or shrubs that have branches that hang down.

Whip A young tree before it develops any side shoots.

Wirework Wires attached on posts used to support plants.

Suppliers

Hand tools A range of tools for pruning are available from local garden centres and hardware stores. In country areas, agricultural merchants also carry a wide selection.

Power tools Power tools for most purposes are available from garden centres and hardware stores. More powerful machines are also available from garden and farm machinery outlets. Better deals may be had by sourcing from the internet,

but local suppliers have the advantage that they may also service the machinery.

One of the biggest suppliers is Stihl and a search of their website (www.stihl.com) will give a list of worldwide suppliers. They can be bought locally and have a network for servicing and repairs.

Tree ties, stakes, string, netting and other sundries
These are available from garden centres, hardware stores and agricultural merchants.

Index

Page numbers in *italic* refer to the illustrations

Acknowledgements

The Publisher would like to thank the following gardens and garden owners for kindly allowing photography to take place on their premises:

Andrew Mikolajski, Northamptonshire; Bedgebury Pinetum, Kent; Batsford Arboretum, Gloucestershire; Brogdale Horticultural Trust, Faversham, Kent; Chenies Manor, Buckinghamshire; Chiffchaffs, Dorset; East Lambrook Manor,

Somerset; Elsing Hall, Norfolk; Headland Garden, Cornwall; Fiona Henley Design; Lamport Hall, Northamptonshire; Merrist Wood, Surrey; Pine Lodge Gardens, Cornwall; Renishaw Hall, Sheffield; RHS Chelsea Flower Show 2004; RHS Hyde Hall, Essex; RHS Gardens Rosemoor, Devon; RHS Gardens Wisley, Surrey; Rodmarton Manor, Cirencester; Spinners, Devon; Westonbirt Arboretum, Gloucestershire; Wollerton Old Hall, Shropshire; Writtle College, Essex;

Wyken Hall, Suffolk; Yalding Organic Gardens, Kent

A special thank you to STIHL Ltd. who kindly lent some of the tools and equipment used in the book. A list of worldwide suppliers that stock Stihl products can be found on their website: www.stihl.com

The Publisher would like to thank the following people for acting as models in photography sessions: Jeff Clayton; Nick Robinson; Peter

Sedgewick; Robin Whitehead; Stephen Coling

The Publisher would also like to thank the following picture libraries for kindly allowing their images to be reproduced in this book:
t = top b = bottom c = centre
l = left r = right
The Garden Picture Library: 14t (Marie O'Hara); 34bl (Jane Legate); 14br (David England); 37bl (Jane Legate. Science Photo Library: 39bl (Paul Shoesmith).